WINNING, Inc.

A Championship
Handbook for
High-Performing
Leaders

JOE BOHRINGER

Winning, Inc.

Copyright © 2025 Joe Bohringer

Published 2025

Printed in the United States of America

10 9 8 7 6 5 4 3 2 1

ISBN-13: 978-1-7348450-9-9 (Paperback)
ISBN-13: 979-8-9988850-1-3 (ebook)
ISBN-13: 979-8-9988850-0-6 (Hardcover)

Cover design by Book Cover Hub
Interior designed by Erin Stocco, Modernbookdesign.com

My deepest love and thanks to Kathleen and Lauren for choosing to come along for the ride.

TABLE OF CONTENTS

INTRODUCTION

"I can't believe you got paid to watch baseball!"

It's true. I did watch baseball, and lots of it. Thousands of games filled with memorable moments. Excited amateurs chasing professional dreams. Proud parents watching Major League debuts. Jubilant dogpiles of playoff victors. As a long-time Major League front office executive, I was fortunate to experience several championships of my own including a World Series. From dusty sandlots to stadium boardrooms, I loved my 31 seasons in Major League Baseball.

But it was not all fun and games. I also lived the business's darker side. The sting of last-place finishes. The devastation of career-ending injuries. The heartbreak of crushing an athlete's dream by telling them their all-out best is simply not good enough. These memories are not as kind.

It is hard to describe the ruthless, high-stakes nature of professional sports. The entire industry is built upon players, coaches, and executives pushing performance to its absolute limit. And when performance falls short, you are quickly cast aside for the next contender. Competition is fierce, feedback is immediate, and the next difficult decision is always right around the corner. Every day is a battle between the urgency to win now and the responsibility to sustain the franchise's long-term health. I didn't just get paid to watch baseball. I got paid to plan, lead, and execute in a distinctly unforgiving environment.

Most fans recognize the stakes for players – get it done or lose your spot. What fewer realize is that sports executives face similar pressures. The four major North American leagues – the National Football League, National Basketball Association, National Hockey League, and my former home of Major League Baseball – have just 124 franchises. That means only 124 top decision-makers, each with the expectation of being the last team standing. Even the best face long odds against the inevitable health, luck, and team unity obstacles between training camp and a championship. Yet each one embraces this grind. Like the athletes they oversee, the best sports executives around the world aren't just high performers but elite performers at their craft.

This environment makes sports an excellent training ground for business leaders. But don't take my word for it. Listen to the experts. Comprehensive studies from universities like Harvard[1], Rhode Island[2], and Britain's Institute of Leadership[3] have long shown that the persistence, resilience, and teamwork traits acquired through competitive athletics strongly correlate with business success. Workplace reports from powerhouse consulting firms like Deloitte, McKinsey, and Ernst & Young say the same.

---

1 *No Revenge for Nerds? Evaluating the Careers of Ivy League Athletes* (Amornsiripanitch, Gompers, Hu, Levinson. and Mukharlyamov) [2023]

2 *Business Leadership Traits Developed by Participation in College Athletics* (Lefebrve) [2014]

3 *Leaders at Play: Game-changing Leadership from Sport to Workplace* (Institute of Leadership & Management) [2017]

Sports executives operate under unyielding pressure to identify the right people, build the right culture, and implement the right systems. All under win-or-else expectations. Every move receives public scrutiny, and every choice has real-time consequences. While some industries measure results over quarters or even years, sports' scoreboard and standings provide immediate results for instant analysis. The feedback loops are short, fast, and brutally honest. The game just doesn't care.

Success in this industry demands continuous improvement. It is a never-ending cycle of questioning assumptions, pushing boundaries, and reinventing yourself to stay ahead of the curve. The further I advanced in my own career, the more I came to appreciate the value of outside perspectives to help navigate that cycle. That led to contacts in other sports leagues around the world.

Over time – and in pursuit of broader knowledge to stay ahead – my network expanded to leaders in more "traditional" industries like consulting, law, psychology, academia, venture capital, and big tech. Most of my initial contacts were former classmates met while earning a business degree at the Massachusetts Institute of Technology. The list grew with connections made while attending conferences, serving on panels, or speaking to groups. I quickly learned pro sports is far from the only field with intense competition and high stakes. In fact, I found high-level leaders across industries use many of the same core strategies for consistent success.

This book represents the best of those strategies. It distills countless conversations and decades of experience into nine battle-tested principles for success in any business setting. These principles provide a blueprint for building a winning environment, establishing winning procedures, and designing support systems for both short-

and long-term success. The final chapter demonstrates how living these principles can achieve extraordinary results:

Principle One: Winning Is Not Normal.

Principle Two: People Drive Process.

Principle Three: Make Championship Demands.

Principle Four: Standards Are Not Negotiable.

Principle Five: Your Culture Is What You Tolerate.

Principle Six: Buy-In Is Not Enough.

Principle Seven: Get Comfortable Being Uncomfortable.

Principle Eight: Master Your Information.

Principle Nine: Wisdom Beats Experience.

The Final Score: Put 'Em All Together.

These principles cover the mindset, staffing, systems, and standards of peak-performing organizations. Each begins with a detailed explanation of the core concept followed by an authentic, behind-the-scenes example. These real-world stories pinpoint the challenges around the principle before leading you through a successful resolution. Each principle concludes with three key questions applying these ideas to your own roadmap for success.

For three decades and counting, I have been privileged to collaborate with and learn from a host of world-class executive leaders. *Winning, Inc.* brings those experiences and insights to you as well. I hope you find them as valuable as I have.

WINNING IS NOT NORMAL

Be prepared to make the commitment.

"Winning isn't normal. That doesn't mean there's anything wrong with winning.
It just isn't the norm. It is highly unusual."

– *Dr. Keith Bell, renowned sports psychologist*

The world is a competitive place. Whether we realize it or not, this lesson is taught from an early age. Playground games. Class elections. College placement exams. All are subtle – and sometimes not so subtle – previews of our adulthood to come. We need to get the job, win that promotion, or keep our businesses afloat when times get tough. Even when the rules aren't quite clear, most of us have no choice but to play the game.

The business of sports is a condensed version of this wider world. In pro sports, "goals" aren't vague ideals that can be hazily pursued but literal measurements of success. And scoreboards grant no nuance. You are either winning or losing for all to see.

While the metrics might vary, businesses also separate their winners from also-rans. Whether measured by revenue, market share, or some other indicator, we generally know which companies are barely hanging on and which dominate their field. In today's world, businesses have more ways than ever to keep score. Traditional financial statements are now joined by increasingly complex OKRs, KPIs, and NPSs. But the core interpretation remains unchanged –

you either reside above or below the line.

While no company promotes striving for average, most end up stubbornly stuck in that range. Why is that? And more importantly, what is it that keeps consistent performers on top? The answer often starts with mindset. While metrics measure *outputs*, everything we know about winning starts with *inputs*. And no input is more important to winning than fully committing in the first place. I've learned firsthand that level of commitment is far from normal.

My biggest lesson on the abnormality of winning came in the fall of 2011. On October 12 that year, Theo Epstein signed a five-year deal to leave the Boston Red Sox for the Chicago Cubs. One of the most successful baseball executives of all time, Theo burst onto the scene in 2002 when the Red Sox made him the youngest General Manager in baseball history at just 28 years old. A Boston native, he was being asked to break "The Curse of the Bambino," the locals' term for decades of disappointment since the ill-fated trade of star player Babe Ruth to the rival New York Yankees in 1920. A key contributor to Boston's last championship in 1918, Ruth went on to become one of the world's most famous athletes while also kickstarting the Yankees to a record 27 world titles. Meanwhile, the Red Sox mostly languished in mediocrity after that bittersweet 1918 win.

Theo quickly showed boldness in the role. He famously traded away star player and fan favorite Nomar Garciaparra believing it would improve the team's chances to win. Unsurprisingly, Red Sox fans were outraged. But the move paid off as Boston not only broke the curse by winning the 2004 World Series but added another in 2007 for good measure.

Theo now faces a similar challenge in Chicago. The Cubs are

mired in an even longer drought, with their last World Series victory coming in 1908. Chicago's lack of success runs so deep the team is nationally known as baseball's "Lovable Losers." The Cubs even have a curse of their own. "The Curse of the Billy Goat" was born in 1945 when the owner of a local tavern and his pet goat were ejected from Chicago's stadium during Game 4 of the World Series. As he left, the owner famously declared the Cubs would never win again. With the obvious "second curse" narrative, Theo's arrival is national news.

Just a few days after the Cubs' announcement, my phone rings. I am a scout for the Arizona Diamondbacks, and General Manager Kevin Towers – affectionately known league wide as "KT" – is on the line. I assume he wants to discuss some players I had reported on during the season, but the topic turns out to be something else entirely.

In baseball, virtually every team employee works under a contract. Not only do players have fixed contracts, but so do coaches, scouts, and front office employees. Major League Baseball's tampering rules are clear: formal permission is required to discuss employment with another organization's employee. The penalties for violation are severe.

KT tells me Theo wants to interview me for the Cubs' Director of Pro Scouting role. That's certainly not what I expected when I picked up the phone.

The Pro Scouting department is vital to any Major League organization. You can't build a championship team without finding championship players, after all. The department tracks hundreds of active Major League players along with thousands more in leagues across North America, Asia, and Latin America. Any recommendation for trades, free agents, or waiver claims heavily involves the Pro Scouting office.

After chatting about the role and my readiness for it, KT finishes with, "You know what Theo's like."

"Actually, I don't," I admit. "I've never met him."

"What?" he says somewhat amused. "Never?!?"

"Never."

There's a pause. Then KT laughs. Hard. "Well, I'll tell you one thing. I'd *love* to be a fly on the wall for that interview."

"Oh? Why's that?"

"Because neither of you pulls any punches."

Thanks for the heads up, KT.

Hanging up is a gut check. I do have a sense where I'd like my career to go. After nearly two decades, I've been fortunate to spend most of my career with winning teams – the industry's simplest standard of success. I experienced deep playoff runs with Pittsburgh and Arizona. I also had a role with a Montreal Expos team that compiled baseball's best record before a player's strike infamously cancelled the 1994 World Series. The common thread in all those stops is the right leaders at the decision-making table. Not a bunch of individuals chasing job titles – of which every industry has plenty – but a cohesive group focused solely on winning decisions. That experience has shifted my ambition away from specific job titles to finding the right table. And I'd rather sit at the foot of the right table than the head of the wrong one. Because if there's one constant in pro sports, sitting at the wrong table eventually gets you fired.

My table theory had been tested the year before when the Pittsburgh Pirates asked to speak to me about a high-level front office role. It's an attractive seat, and I have a prior relationship with Pittsburgh's General Manager. Unfortunately, I left the interview openly wondering if a notoriously stingy ownership group would ever pony up the resources to win. When a contract was presented, I had a dilemma. There are only thirty Major League teams, meaning only thirty slots for most executive roles. Would I really consider walking away from my best opportunity yet to fill one? And with someone I respected and trusted?

One thing I've learned is it's extremely hard to earn one of these positions. Another – which applies here – is if you accept one and don't perform, you might never get a second chance. Was this opportunity legitimate? I didn't fear doing more with less, which is a core requirement for small market teams in any league. However, I did need to believe Pittsburgh's ownership was committed to giving us a fair shot. After an agonizing round of personal and professional discussions, my instincts said that commitment just wasn't there. Having no idea if another opportunity would ever come along, I removed myself from further consideration in Pittsburgh.

Here's another chance. And this is not just any table – it's Theo Epstein's. He knows not only what a championship table looks like but is judge and jury of building one in Chicago. I can guess what that entails, but Theo *knows*. Will it look anything like I expect? Even more unnerving, will Theo think I am capable of holding a seat?

Two days later I pull up to the Cubs' iconic Wrigley Field. Apparently, this rebuild is both figurative and literal. With the offices under renovation, I pass two temporary trailers housing staff in the parking lot. Inside the stadium, we weave around scattered tools and plastic sheeting as the offices are reconfigured for the expected influx of new staff.

Theo, with his newly minted President of Baseball Operations title, is joined by Jed Hoyer, the Cubs' new General Manager. Jed previously worked with Theo in Boston. The early discussion is standard stuff: the job description, my experience, general scouting philosophy, and a video exercise talking through a player evaluation.

As the session continues, the mood tightens. Jed talks less and Theo more. The conversation pivots from superficial items like job responsibilities and scouting mechanics to deeper matters like the traits and expectations of the Cubs' new front office. We are getting down to business.

A few minutes in I ask, "What type of people are you looking for?"

Theo pauses, almost as if he's deciding. His previously thoughtful look hardens to a competitive glare. It is intense, fearless, *relentless*. His words come out low and steady. Of all the quotes from all the anecdotes in this book, this is the one most likely recalled word for word. It was that jarring. It was winning stripped bare.

"I did not come here to fucking lose. Five-year plans are bullshit. I want people who can run a five-year plan in three. Those who can might have a place here. Those who can't, don't."

I had wanted to see what a championship table looked like. Here it was literally staring me in the face. KT was right – no punches pulled indeed. The only thing I know for sure is I want a seat at this table.

I return Theo's gaze, try like hell to sound composed, and reply, "I don't like losing either. That timeline's fine with me."

The details are blurry after this exchange, but I don't think they matter. That was the moment. I either had the job, or I didn't.

Less than a week later, I am introduced as the Cubs' new Director of Pro Scouting. The first year we lose 101 games to finish with the second-worst record in all of baseball. That season is a painful slog for everyone involved. Our team lacks talent, but we knew that coming in. What we signed up for was the hard work of getting better.

That offseason is filled with difficult but honest conversations. Some lead to drastic changes in communication and reporting lines. Others lead to revamped programs, spearheaded by a new end-to-end database managing every available piece of baseball information. Sadly, several conversations result in moving on from popular, long-time staff members who simply do not fit the organization's new direction. One thing is painstakingly clear: "lovable" and "losing" will no longer be permitted to coexist at Wrigley Field.

Three seasons later the Cubs advance to the National League Championship Series, a step short of the World Series. It is an admirable accomplishment by a well-regarded young team, but with unfinished business attached. The following year, the Cubs win a dramatic Game 7 in extra innings to clinch the franchise's first World Series in 108 years. A handful of front office members famously celebrate by eating goat in the Wrigley Field bleachers. And with that, a second curse is broken.

Is winning that simple? Absolutely not, and I do not want to undersell the hard work and sacrifice of *every single member* of the Cubs organization during that span. Winning is hard in any industry, and committing to it that fully invariably creates uncomfortable side effects. Baseball's side effects include thousands of hours spent in ballparks and boardrooms rather than home with family and friends. I'm sure executives in almost any industry can relate.

In this case, it took five seasons for the Cubs to steadily grind from a league worst showing to a championship win. That also happens to be one of the quickest worst-to-first turnarounds in the history of sports. In that respect, I guess you could say it was a heck of a five-year plan.

Except it never was a five-year plan, and that's the point. That one interview exchange set the mindset for the entire journey. The tone came not just from Theo's words, but also the look on his face as he delivered them. There was zero lip service. It was the real deal. From day one, we would relentlessly challenge the status quo to find a better way. That meant every person, program, and philosophy would be measured against a championship standard. Anything less was unacceptable. To everyone's credit, the group never wavered. The Cubs, the fans, and the city of Chicago celebrated as a result.

The first step to winning – in any industry – is never a physical act. It's the mental understanding that winning is not normal. Normal is average. Normal is comfortable. Winning is anything but. Winners must be prepared to face the grind. They understand setbacks are part of the game. But most importantly, winners accept that if they are not willing to do the work, they likely won't win at all.

Winning is not a moment but a mindset – a mindset that must be embraced before the journey even begins.

KEY QUESTIONS TO CONSIDER:

- What is your "win"?

- What environment do you need to create to seize that opportunity?

- How willing are you to fully embrace the mindset needed to produce your winning outcome?

READER NOTES

PEOPLE DRIVE PROCESS

Great outcomes require great people.

"People are not your most important asset. The right people are."

— *Jim Collins, renowned author and speaker*

People and process – every business needs both. When in sync, they can propel us to new heights, and out of sorts they can cause our demise. Yet despite the fundamental connection, their contributions are far from equal. While process is vital to any outcome, it is people who ultimately drive our success.

I wish I had known this sooner in my career. Like many executives, I spent my early years obsessed with process. It seemed the smartest and quickest way to lead a team. I was constantly examining and tweaking systems to squeeze out marginal performance gains.

In many ways, this is an easier leadership style. We know people matter, but process never talks back. Or disagrees with your opinion. Or has a bad day at home before coming to the office. Tweaking process almost always feels productive. Confronting someone holding us back? Not so much. But while effective tweaks can yield incremental gains, the ability to find, develop, and inspire the right people can transform an organization.

Think of it this way: if you take a great process and surround it with poor people, it will become a poor process. Poor people will drag it to their level. Conversely, pairing poor process with great people does exactly the opposite. Great people simply won't stand for a poor process, and if given enough time will create a great process instead.

The higher the competition, the more people become the deciding factor. A good process can cover flaws and keep you afloat for quite a while. At the highest levels though, people win championships.

Sorting through stories for this principle, I was reminded of several people who singlehandedly improved our organization's process. However – and I begrudgingly admit this – my best example is a person who almost drove our process off a cliff.

In 2016, I am offered the chance to leave the Chicago Cubs for a larger role with the Seattle Mariners. A few weeks earlier, an ownership group unhappy with the team's performance fired the previous General Manager and hired Jerry Dipoto for the job. I came aboard a short time later as Special Assistant to the General Manager. The Mariners hadn't made the postseason in fifteen years, one of the longest current non-playoff streaks in professional sports. While there's no catchy curse name attached, the initial landscape in Seattle is very similar to what I encountered in Chicago.

In business terms, it is your typical change management overhaul. Ownership has decided it wants a fundamentally different approach, and our new leadership team is being asked to lead that effort. The mandate is simple: win more games.

For us, "people and process" is not just a concept. It becomes our mantra. Coined and most frequently used by new Director of Player Development Andy McKay, the philosophy revolves around finding the right balance between the two. Unfortunately to start, the Mariners sit behind the industry curve in the more influential part of the equation – its people.

Like most industries, sports is a copycat business. The easiest perceived shortcut for improving a struggling firm is hiring someone from a successful competitor. Earlier I described baseball's strict permission policy for interviewing employees from other organizations. We learn shortly after arrival the Mariners haven't received a permission ask for a coach, scout, or front office employee in over five years. That's an awful long time for an entire industry to ignore your people pipeline, so improving that pipeline becomes a priority.

In fairness, the Mariners' compensation policies play a role. Unlike the big-market Cubs, Seattle is a midmarket franchise with very cost-conscious ownership. As such, most staff salaries rank in the middle-to-bottom third of the league, and new job openings are routinely funded at or near the bottom of the scale. This is not a criticism. It is simply context for the Mariners' business model, one they still employ today.

Companies using this model typically find two types of hires: experienced candidates with lesser talent or talented candidates with lesser experience. In an industry where talent matters as much as professional sports, midmarket teams hoping to win have little choice but to take the unproven talent – whether player or staff – and hope to develop it. I've once heard leadership described as either extracting performance or unlocking potential. I think that's exactly right. In Seattle, we are all-in on unlocking potential.

The cornerstone of that effort is an active learning and development program. We keep written manuals as short as possible in favor of hands-on education. We hold interactive workshops, design targeted field work, and pair less-experienced staff with mentors where possible. We also assign joint projects encouraging collaboration and relationship building across departments. The entire curriculum is geared to promote individual growth while also giving exposure to other areas of the operation.

Most of our early attention is paid to the scouting department. This is by design since scouts are our first filter for bringing new players into the organization. Over the first couple years in Seattle, we make considerable progress. We are improving our processes while adding talent to our staff. Our younger scouts and analysts are finding their voices, and the Mariners' steady climb up industry rankings of minor league players suggest our efforts are seeing results. However, we still have one stumbling block: our amateur draft room.

The amateur draft is a pivotal event in every sport. It is an annual opportunity to add young players who can shape a franchise's future. However, the unproven nature of these players – many of them still high school age – makes them among the riskiest acquisitions in the game. It is sports' version of hiring a gaggle of hotshot business-school grads who haven't actually accomplished anything yet in the real world. Such imperfect information makes ranking these prospects inherently subjective. It also means differences in opinion are guaranteed to arise.

Like most of us, scouts are territorial. They spend months and sometimes years getting to know not just a player's skills but the character, work ethic, and intangibles behind them. That often makes it hard for scouts to separate themselves from the players they believe in. Helping unearth a possible All-Star or Hall of Famer is the ultimate scouting badge of honor.

Roughly two weeks before the draft, each team gathers its key evaluators to whittle down hundreds of names to the twenty or so who will be selected. From a business perspective, picture gathering dozens of Project Managers after months or even years of very personal work to determine which tiny handful of proposals will continue and which will get the axe. Now imagine packing all that passion, bias, and ego into one room to debate what stays and what goes. It's a recipe for intense, emotionally charged deliberations. That's the draft room, and I am sure any experienced leader can relate to the potential for disaster.

Our VP of Scouting, Tom Allison, has a great phrase for this dilemma. Tommy has run dozens of draft meetings, and he starts every single one with a reminder on the importance of "disagreeing without being disagreeable." In a combustible environment like the draft, walking this line is the difference between constructive conversation and disruptive argument. In simpler terms, it is the difference between success and failure.

Unfortunately, one of our long-time scouts has zero interest in the concept. Even worse, this scout has some of the best pure instincts on our staff. He is a former player, coach, and manager who at his best brings valuable perspective to any industry conversation. At his worst though, watch out. Despite several attempts, his prickly nature has made him unreliable in any teaching or mentoring role. And yes, he's received plenty of candid feedback along the way.

In Seattle, we have a practice of inviting other departments to observe our first few draft discussions. It is a great opportunity for Mariner business employees to get a glimpse of team operations. It's also a chance for scouts normally scattered throughout the country to mingle with home city teammates they would otherwise never meet. It is a thoughtful gesture normally benefitting everyone as the discussion settles in.

Except this year's discussion is unsettled right from the start. Calling our malcontent disagreeable would be too kind. Scorched earth is more appropriate. He exaggerates the strengths of players he likes while belittling others getting similar consideration. Positive attributes are sarcastically dismissed, and objective measures outright ignored. Worst of all is his open disdain for differing opinions.

Of the couple dozen draft rooms I've attended, this is by far the worst. It's a toxic atmosphere contrary to everything we stand for, and it is all being sabotaged by a single participant. No matter how much our process has improved, we are on the verge of losing our people. Experienced voices are being drowned out while younger voices are afraid to speak up. Half the room is shutting down rather than engage in a no-win verbal wrestling match.

This scout's need to *be* right is overriding any consideration to *do* right on behalf of the organization. Ultimately though, doing right by the organization is the whole point. If our final decisions are going to be browbeaten by a single person, why bother bringing everyone together in the first place?

The situation is barely manageable, and the sour taste is everywhere as the draft concludes. With so much successful groundwork at risk, the next move is obvious. We cannot continue letting one individual undermine the entire team no matter how useful his knowledge or expertise might be in saner moments. Before the season even ends, we inform this scout his contract will not be renewed.

But just because a move is obvious doesn't make it easy. No leader wants to send someone home to his or her family having lost their livelihood. However, the harsh reality of pro sports is if you can't deliver that message when needed, the family eventually hearing the bad news will be yours.

Once the move is made, the improvement of our next few meetings is startling. Established evaluators show renewed energy. Younger ones more creativity. Opinions increase, information improves, and the quality of our conversations deepens across the board. Best of all, our scouts and analysts begin collaborating in a way that elevates the entire group. Removing one toxic presence unlocks the potential of a dozen others almost overnight. This includes multiple people who admittedly prove to be more capable of driving process than we initially thought.

The next season is a revelation. The budding relationships feed off each other, and multiple people take huge strides in performance and responsibility. Once word trickles out, the permission asks from other teams start trickling in. We suddenly see promising staff earning well-deserved recognition for turning upside into execution. It is a welcome change and a testament to our staff development program. By the time I leave Seattle before the 2021 season, we regularly receive permission asks from competitors looking to bolster their own staffs. But those asks never happen if we hadn't created an environment allowing that growth in the first place.

Regardless of industry, we all recognize the need for talent on our teams. At the same time, every organization has talented individuals who just aren't good teammates. Renowned speaker Simon Sinek refers to them as High Performance/Low Trust employees – the ones everyone instantly points to when asked, "Who's the asshole?".

It's the tantalizing talent of these employees that disguises the pitfall. Almost every leader in this situation – and by extension every leadership team – believes they can extract the positive while containing the negative. First, we all know how hard it is to find difference-making talent. Second, isn't the hard work of managing people a basic responsibility of leadership?

So, how do we decide whether to attempt converting a talented agitator? And how long should we stick with it when we do? My experience has been the experiment's only worthwhile as long as that person's contributions (and hopefully behavioral adjustments) are not impeding organizational progress. The instant that changes is the instant to consider moving on. As the above example shows, both your process and *more importantly your remaining people* will improve as a result. Given the relationship between the two, it's the best chance of letting your people drive your process to new heights.

KEY QUESTIONS TO CONSIDER:

- Who are the right people to drive your organization's process?

- What type of support or environment do they need to succeed?

- How well are you aligning your people and processes to make sure they compound each other rather than conflict?

READER NOTES

MAKE CHAMPIONSHIP DEMANDS

Elite results start with elite behaviors.

"Champions behave like champions
before they're champions."

– Bill Walsh, Hall of Fame football coach

Championships are never won overnight. They are earned one small, painstaking step at a time. Every iconic company starts as the flicker of an idea. Every legendary CEO was once an entry-level employee. We celebrate the names, but how did they get there?

Much of the commentary to date focuses on tactics. Books on executives rising to the top through strategy and communication. Or case studies on corporations becoming household names through excellence in operations, innovation, or customer relations. Once you identify your tactical niche, there are multiple avenues for success.

But tactics alone don't build champions. The biggest winners also show consistent behaviors – actions inspired by passion, resilience, and a willingness to take risks. These are at the heart of this chapter. As with tactics, no single set of behaviors guarantees success. Yet every organization has an optimal mix. The key is identifying the behaviors most relevant to your situation and steadfastly incorporating them into everything you do. These become your foundation for championship performance.

My biggest exposure to the behaviors required for a championship foundation occurred during my first few months in Chicago. During a cold November about a week after joining the Cubs, I am sitting at lunch with two junior staffers at a restaurant near Wrigley Field. Both have been with the Cubs a few seasons, and Chicago has been their only professional stop so far. I'll call them Rob and James for this account.

As we wait for our food, the televisions are replaying the previous night's National Hockey League highlights. Onscreen we see a player with blood streaming down his face after being hit by a puck.

Rob quickly turns to James.

"Would you take a puck to the face for a World Series ring?"

James thinks a moment, "Yeah, I'd do that."

He then counters to Rob, "Would you take one to the nuts?"

Rob winces. "Am I wearing a cup?"

"Nah, too easy. No cup."

After another pause, Rob shakes his head. "No. I don't think I would do that."

No doubt seeing my confused expression, they fill me in. Apparently, this game is a running joke in the Cubs front office. It started a couple years earlier at the Baseball Winter Meetings. The Winter Meetings are an annual December event where all thirty teams gather with hundreds of media, agents, players, and fans to conduct business for the upcoming season. For those familiar with the lingo, it's the Hot Stove at its hottest as far as trade discussions and free agent deals. Each team headquarters its staff in a large suite where they can come together for strategy sessions. Unsurprisingly, after long hours in tight quarters, those sessions sometimes stray off-topic.

At this one, the Cubs' contingent ends a long day with an open bar in their suite. The conversation turns to, "What would you do for a World Series ring?" Chicago hadn't won one in over a century after all. As the alcohol flows, so do the suggestions and pledges. Each gets more absurd than the last. Silently watching is one of the baseball administrators. She is quiet, mild-mannered, middle-aged. When she speaks at all, you have to lean in to hear. Picture a librarian who just happens to work for a baseball team.

After several rounds of one-upmanship by the rest of the crew, she unexpectedly – and quite boastfully – vows to engage in inappropriate acts with a well-known member of the stadium cleaning crew. It's ridiculous, vulgar, and wildly out of character for the person saying it. It is also hilarious. Her pledge not only wins the night but keeps the entire group in stitches the remainder of the meetings. I have only worked with this group for a week, but even I see the humor when matching the promise with the person who made it.

When the story is finished, they seem pleased. James leans back and says, "So, what would *you* do for a World Series ring?"

I look at him flatly and say, "I'd get better players."

They stare at me like I am speaking a foreign language. Maybe I am, but it's the honest answer.

"We don't work in Ticket Sales or Media Relations," I continue. "We're Baseball Operations. We have complete control over the team that goes on the field. We don't need to play hypothetical games about what we'd do to win a World Series ring. We can just get better players."

They sit stunned. I can see on their faces they've never strayed too far down this line of thinking before, at least out loud. We're the Cubs. We aren't expected to win, and these two are acting like that's our predetermined fate. I know the new leadership team has no intention of behaving that way. Neither do I. As part of that leadership, I feel responsible for making sure Rob and James know as well.

When our food arrives, we decide to keep playing. By the time we leave, their World Series ideas are much more practical. And to be honest, they aren't bad. Their frontline perspective immediately identifies areas we can better communicate with staff in the field. It's not that they have no insight into creating winning behaviors. It's just that they've never been asked this candidly before. Well, they are being asked now, and their excitement is unmistakable. It's a small step, but definitely one in the right direction.

That small step becomes a larger one the following February. At the start of spring training, roughly two hundred Cubs' non-playing employees gather in Arizona for an organizational meeting. It is our first under Theo Epstein.

As we file into the auditorium, I take a seat next to Billy Blitzer, a scout who's been with the Cubs more than 30 years. A member of my pro scouting staff, Billy is Brooklyn personified – thick accent, straightforward talk, and a deep love of baseball. Most of his career has been spent watching amateur players up and down the US Eastern seaboard. He's spent the last few years on the professional side evaluating minor league and Major League players.

In the opening session, Theo lays out his expectations in no uncertain terms: "Be better than the other 29." For most jobs, thirty MLB franchises means thirty roles. Whether you are the Cubs' Major League shortstop, Texas-based scout, or office assistant at the Dominican Republic academy, you have 29 industry peers. Theo firmly asserts the fastest way for the Cubs to get better is for each individual to focus their actions on nothing more than outperforming their industry peers. No worrying about another department's business. No getting distracted by industry chatter. Just put your head down and "dominate" – his exact word – your competition. The more people who did, the faster the Cubs would improve. Being better than the other 29 will be a key behavioral building block in pursuing an eventual championship.

General Manager Jed Hoyer follows. Jed's message is simple math. We need to get to the playoffs before we can win a World Series. He shows a slide illustrating that since Chicago's last title in 1908, the franchise has made the postseason thirteen times with zero titles. More relevant to baseball's current landscape, the Cubs are 0-for-6 in title chances since the league's move to new divisions and expanded playoffs in 1969.

Meanwhile, the New York Yankees have appeared in 50 postseasons since 1908 and captured 27 World Series titles. The Yankees' record since the 1969 realignment is 21 playoffs with seven championships. In roughly fifteen short minutes, Jed neatly sums up the difference between baseball's best-known winners and the franchise that has spent most of its existence as "Lovable Losers." The message is clear. The playoffs are a crapshoot in every sport, but to have any chance at all, you need to get there first. As Jed phrases it, the first milestone in a championship run is securing a postseason berth. From this point on, everything we do will be measured against that goal. Another well-defined building block.

As we break for lunch, Billy grabs me by the arm and steers me gently aside. He looks troubled as he glances around to make sure we are alone.

"You know," he starts, "I've been to thirty of these meetings, and I don't think I've *ever* heard anyone use 'Cubs' and 'World Series' in the same sentence. The only time we heard 'World Series' was if we were talking about the team that just won it."

He pauses, then shakes his head disbelievingly, "Theo and Jed said it *like every other sentence!*"

Being honest, Billy looks a little sick to his stomach.

Recalling my first interaction with Theo, I say, "Billy, I don't know much, but I know this: Theo and Jed did not come here to lose. I think we're going to hear 'Cubs' and 'World Series' together a lot the next few days. We should probably get used to it."

Billy stays silent a moment, then breaks into a wide grin. "You know what? That's fine by me."

His reaction isn't a building block. It is more like a building block cementing into place.

That message dominates – there's that word again – the rest of the meeting. The entire discussion focuses on two ideas and two ideas only: being best in class and competing for championships. It is an admittedly high bar, but the bar is not up for debate. Plain and simple, every behavior we encourage and action we take would be measured against a championship standard. That's the challenge, but it is also our opportunity. If we happen to fall short, we are expected to pick ourselves up and do it again until we get it right. It is a message everyone understands. More importantly, it is a message everyone embraces. Now it is up to the organization to follow through with the leadership, support, and resources to make it happen.

Obviously, no championship is won in a single meeting. However, *every* interaction is a chance to move a group closer to that goal. In this interaction, Theo and Jed explicitly defined expected behaviors in Major League Baseball's championship context. Any leader in any industry can do the same. The opportunity lies in identifying your most relevant behaviors and relentlessly making them your reality.

Can any team – or any company – make this transformation, even if its own history suggests otherwise? Absolutely. Just ask Apple. Or Netflix. Or better yet ask Billy, Rob, or James. They were part of a transformation which eventually led to World Series rings.

KEY QUESTIONS TO CONSIDER:

- Who are the "champions" of your industry?

- What are the crucial and often non-negotiable behaviors driving their success?

- Which of these behaviors apply and *more importantly can be implemented* in your own environment?

READER NOTES

STANDARDS ARE NOT NEGOTIABLE

You either meet them or you don't.

"Some people aren't used to an environment where excellence is expected."

— *Steve Jobs, Apple founder*

Every organization says it strives for some form of the following:

- Get the right people.
- Build the right culture.
- Do the right things.

So simple in theory, but history shows how few organizations master all three. It's not that these concepts are flawed. It's that we constantly trip up on the endless and often conflicting interpretations of "right." While data helps immensely in quantifying the right things, people and culture remain tougher nuts to crack.

But the more subjective nature of people-and-culture *data* doesn't mean we lack constructive people-and-culture *information*. Most companies have a wealth of wisdom, knowledge, and experience to help define "right" even if the definition is somewhat broad. For example, we almost always know the difference between good and bad. Likewise, a consensus on average, above average, and below average is rarely difficult. We don't need perfect metrics to set expectations. We just need to agree upon the standards to use as our benchmark.

Why do standards matter? Because in any higher-stakes environment, we are either chasing a bar or raising one. *Every* level of achievement has standards attached, and standards never lower themselves to meet our performance. We must always raise our performance to meet higher standards. We know this instinctively, but that doesn't ease the discomfort when we aren't sure if we measure up. If your goal is to win though, you have no choice but to eventually judge yourself against a winning standard.

Being willing to accept that judgment can be enlightening. I once saw this firsthand when a seemingly innocent question turned into an unplanned exercise on group accountability.

One of the first responsibilities of any new leadership team is the education and implementation of new programs. That is certainly the case when we arrive in Seattle. Combined with a youth movement meant to improve the Mariners' talent pool, our education program takes on even greater emphasis.

A regular feature of this program is group discussions to build alignment. This particular session is a multi-day scouting meeting reviewing our grading scale, reporting process, and information management system. About halfway through the meeting is a question-and-answer forum chaired by a panel of senior leaders and experienced evaluators. It's an opportunity for our staff in the field to go off-script and discuss the topics that matter most to them. I sit with a handful of others on the panel.

Partway through, Jeff Sakamoto raises his hand. A former player and Economics major at Oregon State, Jeff is our scout covering the Pacific Northwest. The local scout for any Major League team operates under a little extra scrutiny, and Jeff represents the Mariners well. He's curious, business-minded, and asks good questions.

On this day Jeff asks, "How do we know if we are one of the top scouts in our territory?"

He is young enough to have plenty of career left but experienced enough to start wondering where he stands. It is a good question. An honest one. And perfect for this forum.

The first few answers reference the logistics of the job. Be on time with your reports. Make sure your schedule gets you to the right ballparks. Expand your coaching contacts to build a better network.

The next few focus on providing quality information to team decision makers. Study the grading scale. Know which analytics best augment your live observations. Don't be afraid to ask your supervisor in the field or teammates in the front office when you need help.

It's all good advice, but none of it fully answers Jeff's question. He didn't ask how you know if you are an efficient scout or one who is helpful to management. He asked how you know if you are one of the top scouts in your territory.

When the conversation turns to me, I say, "Good question. I always tried to gauge where I stood against the top scouts in my area. We all know our main competition. I judged myself against that."

A sawed-off version of Theo Epstein's "be better than the other 29" message pops into my head...and then right out of my mouth.

"You know all the scouts in your territory, right?"

"Yup."

"Okay. Who are the top three? I don't need names. Just the three scouts who when you walk into the ballpark, you think 'uh oh, I better be prepared to work today'."

I see Jeff mulling it over.

"You have them?"

"Yes."

Forming my next sentence, I suddenly realize this is no longer a one-on-one conversation. I zoom out and see Jeff isn't the only scout thinking. They all are. I can see the math going on in their heads. It wasn't my intention, but Jeff's question is now a 50-person exercise. Any scout with even a few months' experience knows their main rivals. After all, pro sports is literally built around competition. You can't help but know.

This forum might have become a bit more pointed than intended, but there's no turning back now. Jeff asked a professionally honest question. He deserves a professionally honest answer.

"Great," I continue. "Now, if I went to those three scouts and asked them the same exact question…would you make their list?"

I pause to let the question sink in. "That's how I would judge whether you're one of the top scouts in your area."

The look on Jeff's face speaks volumes. He isn't Top 3 yet, but his crossed arms and thoughtful nod say he gets the point. Even better, the glint in his eyes suggests he doesn't fear the challenge.

The other looks in the room run the gamut. A couple flash the quiet confidence of knowing they are well-positioned. Several mirror Jeff, which is not at all surprising given the relative youth of our staff. The surprise is the unsettling number unable to make eye contact at all. Their glances dart between the ceiling, the floor, and even the exit to the room. One poor soul looks like he's about to throw up on his shoes. It is a striking moment.

One simple but honest question has unexpectedly turned into an impromptu 50-person job review. Except management isn't delivering the assessment. These scouts are reviewing themselves under standards entirely of their own making. The only parameter is "Top 3" or roughly the top 10% of their own peers. As far as reviews go, it is hard to fool yourself when you are running both ends of the conversation.

I have since seen this "review yourself" exercise work in multiple industries. And when introduced properly, participants unfailingly know which standards apply. They just need a method for framing them.

In the business world, I have yet to meet a top executive who doesn't lean into this drill. You simply have them apply a basic 1-to-10 scale to any important issue where exact metrics do not exist. For any response below ten, the obvious follow up becomes the route to a higher grade. What are the easiest or quickest ways to move one number higher? Likewise, what are the biggest, boldest steps you can take to emphatically close the gap between your current number and a 10?

These two questions create a powerful framework for improvement. The first identifies smaller, shorter-term wins to keep your teams motivated and engaged. The second helps identify the major, longer-term initiatives that can move your organization to new heights.

And if your current grade is a 10? Well, keep doing what you're doing. That said, I have yet to meet the top executive who believes perfection is possible. While most execs aren't afraid to venture toward the top of the scale, they *always* leave room for improvement. That is part of what's made them successful in the first place.

Deep down inside, most of us know exactly where we stand. We also know the "right" standards to apply. Our next level of success doesn't come from creating new standards. It simply requires acknowledging and meeting the standards we already know exist.

KEY QUESTIONS TO CONSIDER:

- What are the non-negotiable standards you know must be met to reach your personal or organizational goals?

- On a scale of 1-to-10, how well are you currently meeting those standards?

- What are the initial steps – both small and large – you can take toward reaching your next level of performance?

READER NOTES

PRINCIPLE FIVE
YOUR CULTURE IS WHAT YOU TOLERATE

So don't take any bullshit.

"The culture of any organization is shaped by the worst behavior the leader is willing to tolerate."

– from School Culture Rewired *by Steve Gruenert and Todd Whitaker*

"We're going to work hard and work smart!"

Every leader says it, and every organization promotes it. In sports, every team promises to outwork its opponents. Every player is going to give it their all. And every front office claims it will turn cutting-edge analytics into a competitive edge.

Business is no different. Every firm sets out to constructively collaborate, efficiently execute, and optimally optimize. Yet with such clear goals, why do so few organizations pull it off? In most cases, it's the difference between words and actions.

Anyone can talk about excellence, but our true cultures lie in how we react when someone falls short of those goals. A sports culture is defined by what happens when a team *doesn't* work hard, a player *doesn't* give it their all, or a front office clings to redundant or outdated processes. In theory, these stumbles are addressed immediately. In reality, we too often find ways to rationalize these flaws. We label them as one-time mistakes or avoid conversations we know are needed to correct course. When that avoidance becomes routine, our one-time events become recurring habits that quietly kill our hard-and-smart culture.

The same applies to business. How do we react when collaboration is stalled by selfish employees, execution slips due to outdated processes, or optimization is ruined by sloppy work? Like it or not, your responses to these scenarios become your culture's defining moments.

Our stated cultures are *never* true unless our words are backed by reinforcing behaviors. Success is not just saying it. It's living it. And that means having the courage to identify and address behaviors that fall short of our cultural standards.

I learned this firsthand during one of the most turbulent transitions in sports history. The 1990s saw a wave of family-owned sports franchises sold to large corporations as soaring media rights flooded leagues with billions in new revenue. It was a seminal time in the evolution of pro sports into big business.

Nowhere was this evolution more dramatic than Los Angeles, where media behemoths Disney and Fox engaged in an epic battle over programming rights in one of the world's biggest media markets. Disney struck first by buying the National Hockey League's Mighty Ducks of Anaheim and the ESPN all-sports media network. It capped the spree with the purchase of baseball's Anaheim Angels from the family of famous Hollywood entertainer Gene Autry. Beginning with an immediate $100 million stadium renovation, Disney set out to aggressively reposition the Angels in a market traditionally dominated by the nearby Los Angeles Dodgers.

The Dodgers were still a family-run operation, owned by the O'Malley family since 1933. Over the next six decades, the Dodgers pioneered a slew of baseball innovations including MLB's initial West Coast expansion. By the mid-'90s, however, the rest of the league had caught up while the Dodgers stagnated. A wave of modern teams with deep-pocketed corporate owners had eliminated many of the Dodgers' traditional advantages. Los Angeles owner Peter O'Malley admitted as much by stating "groups or corporations are probably the way of the future" given the game's rapidly changing economics.

Those economics finally toppled the Dodgers in 1997. While Disney owned the Angels' broadcasting rights, Fox controlled Dodger games on its Fox Sports West network. In a preemptive move before those rights expired, Fox approached the O'Malley family about purchasing the team. The O'Malleys listened. In September of that year, Fox purchased the Dodgers for a then unheard-of $350 million dollars. Make no mistake though. Running a team was not Fox's priority. The company simply wanted guaranteed media rights to a premier team in one of the world's largest media markets. The franchises themselves were just pawns in the game. The purchase agreement included Peter O'Malley staying on as team President, but the die had been cast. Take that, Disney.

Fox proved to be aggressively active owners. Just a few months into the purchase, Fox executives bypassed O'Malley's holdover baseball leadership to engineer a blockbuster trade with the Florida Marlins. The players going to Florida included fan favorite and future Hall of Famer Mike Piazza. One of baseball's best players, Piazza had not only spent his entire career in Los Angeles but had close personal ties to former manager and Dodger icon Tommy Lasorda. Fans and media unanimously blasted Fox's corporate overlords for the move.

A month later, Fox unceremoniously fired O'Malley's entire baseball leadership group in a move national media dubbed the "Sunday Night Massacre" for the way it was handled. The departures included General Manager Fred Claire, who had been with the Dodgers for thirty years. At the end of that first season, O'Malley abruptly resigned. It was uncharacteristic chaos for what had previously been one of baseball's most stable franchises.

Fox quickly named a new President and hired Kevin Malone as General Manager in charge of the on-field product. In a surprise to many, Malone had no history in Los Angeles. He came to the Dodgers from the Baltimore Orioles, where he served as a senior executive. Before that, Malone had been General Manager of a Montreal Expos team widely regarded as one of the best run in baseball. Malone's mandate is simple – to shepherd the Dodgers into MLB's corporate age.

Malone's initial Los Angeles impression is not a good one. The local and national media are already hostile toward Fox. Writers lament the switch from the accessible, easygoing O'Malley to a group portrayed as corporate villains. Many long-time Dodger employees feel the same. Malone only adds fuel to the fire by jokingly declaring himself "a new sheriff in town" at his introductory press conference. So much for winning hearts and minds.

In fairness, Malone's inexperience with big market media contributes to the gaffe. A soft-spoken family man at heart, Malone is known for tongue-in-cheek quips delivered in an easy Southern drawl. That folksiness played well in Montreal where any Expos headlines were buried deep beneath the rabid coverage of hockey's Montreal Canadians. In Los Angeles though, Malone's words are taken at face value, which only heightens the growing discomfort with Fox's business style.

One of Malone's first moves upon arriving in L.A. is reuniting with Montreal player development executive Bill Geivett. Geivett hires a 28-year-old from Montreal's top affiliate as a Player Development Assistant. That 28-year-old is me, and excitement aside I have just signed on for whatever Fox and its new sheriff have in mind.

My onboarding is fast and furious. The first assignment is helping Fox's newly appointed CFO audit the club's development programs. It doesn't take long to find disconnects with not only industry standards but the team's internal systems themselves. Like most companies, the Dodgers issue corporate credit cards for travel expenses. The cards are traditionally assigned to each minor league team's travel coordinator. The O'Malleys, however, issue cards to both the travel coordinator and field manager at each stop. The manager cards are littered with questionable charges. One has dozens of "staff meeting about players" at restaurants around the league. Since staff also receive a travel per diem, the double dipping is blatant. While the O'Malleys looked the other way, Fox is having none of it. They consider the cheating a fireable offense but aren't prepared to take such a drastic step so early on. Instead, the managers' cards are taken away.

The backlash is predictable. Returning staff howl at the move, especially a pair of coaches who just happen to be the most shameless abusers. Both are popular former players from past Dodger World Series winners, and both complain loudly to anyone who will listen. We come to learn that both are also angry at being passed over for spots on the Major League coaching staff in a decision made long before Malone arrived. They view the extra meals as a way to make up the difference between their minor league salaries and what they would have made on the Major League staff. Both have guaranteed contracts for the upcoming year, and as stated earlier Fox is hesitant to make any further waves by firing popular former players. We have no choice but to manage the situation as best we can.

Operationally, the audit uncovers an even deeper issue: seriously outdated teaching programs. Baseball's model has evolved from individual managers dictating instruction at each minor league team to an organization-led approach creating customized plans for each player. These plans stick with players regardless of location, drastically improving teaching consistency. This is baseball's working smart, but the Dodgers are stubbornly stuck in an obsolete approach. Even the team's video equipment varies from level to level, making it difficult to track player progress.

These aren't just hiccups around the edges. These are fundamental failures leaving the team at a competitive disadvantage. Regardless of how anyone making changes might be viewed, it is a subpar and unsustainable status quo.

With the audit complete, Geivett begins installing an organization-led approach. Initial details are laid out to the staff in a series of offseason conference calls. The biggest adjustment will be the influence of minor league managers on player instruction. Going forward managers will need collaborative approval for modifying plans rather than making unilateral decisions on their own. Everyone on the calls – both old and new – knows most MLB clubs use this model, but that doesn't make the messaging any easier. Returning staff grumble at the reduced authority, and some insist the changes will not work. Once again, the pair of popular holdovers are the loudest dissenters. In their opinion, these new programs are simply not "The Dodger Way" even though that "way" is roughly a decade out of date.

The conference calls run the better part of ten weeks. The general format reviews information and then opens the discussion to questions and comments. Most staff recognize the need for change, and several make excellent suggestions for improving the transition. Unfortunately, these suggestions are overshadowed by a smaller group rallying behind the two ringleaders resisting change. Despite our best efforts, the number of side conversations and back-channel complaints only increases as the offseason progresses. That underlying tension follows the group into our first spring training camp under Malone.

That camp will be led by chief instructor Rick Sofield. A new hire himself, Rick's top priority is implementing the revamped development program. I assist with planning and materials. As with any new initiative, communication and alignment will be key. Once everyone arrives, our conference calls are replaced by daily staff meetings starting at 8:00 a.m.

On day one, a group of sixty or so bustles in. The room buzzes with the usual first day excitement except for a notable omission. Neither of our dissenting pair has arrived. Rick briefly delays the start while they leisurely stroll in, then covers the day's events. When the meeting ends, he reminds the pair of the scheduled start time.

On day two, we again gather at 8:00 a.m. The pair again saunters in late, but this time Rick has started without them. They noisily shuffle to the back of the room and settle in. Childish for sure, but the standoff is clear. They do not agree with how things are being run. The tardiness is again addressed post-meeting, this time in a firmer tone.

Day three is the inflection point. At 7:59 a.m., the room is full except for the same two coaches. The previous days' bustle is now tense anticipation. The moment is obvious. New management says these meetings matter. Two prominent and influential holdovers are emphatically showing they feel otherwise. Rick has stressed being on time, but the message is being ignored. It is time to decide whether the offending behavior will be tolerated. If the start time doesn't matter, why bother with the rest of the meeting?

At exactly 8:00, Rick stands up, calmly walks over, and locks the door. Then he begins the meeting. At roughly 8:02, the door handle rattles. Rick ignores it and continues speaking. A few seconds later, a sharp knock is heard. Several heads anxiously turn, but Rick keeps going. About 30 seconds later, a closed fist pounds on the door. Rick casually sticks to the day's review. The pounding stops. The meeting continues. Message delivered.

Afterward, Sofield finds the two for a brief recap of the day's plan. Anyone within eyeshot is glued to the showdown even if they have no chance to hear what is being said. An animated discussion ends with Rick informing them tomorrow's meeting will start promptly at 8:00 a.m.

The next day might be the earliest an entire group arrives for the start of a meeting in baseball history. The audience includes our wayward pair. From that day forward, morning meetings start on time. They aren't always comfortable, but they are certainly focused. And as a pleasant side effect, more attention is paid to the larger message as well. While plenty of work remains, it is no longer up for debate whether the Dodgers will move toward the organization-led approach the industry requires. The only question now is how quickly it can be executed.

New management always means new programs. New programs always mean new behaviors. The resulting culture – whatever that might be – is always a reflection of how well those behaviors are introduced, implemented, and ultimately reinforced.

Whether by crisis moments or everyday occurrences, our stated cultures are constantly tested. Our true culture comes from how we handle these tests. When a behavior is clearly detrimental, do we continue to tolerate it or insist on change? We often say we don't have a choice in these situations. Wrong. We do. As Hall of Fame football coach Bill Walsh once stated, "Champions behave like champions before they are champions." That includes choosing what non-championship behaviors you will allow your culture to tolerate.

KEY QUESTIONS TO CONSIDER:

- What behavior is your organization tolerating that you know hinders your desired culture?
- What change in strategy, operations, or expectations would eliminate this behavior?
- How do you best design, implement, and support this change so the offending behavior is no longer an issue?

READER NOTES

BUY-IN IS NOT ENOUGH

Build believe-in instead.

Luke Skywalker: "I don't believe it."

Yoda: "That is why you fail."

— dialogue from Star Wars: The Empire Strikes Back

"**B**uy-in" is one of the most popular topics in leadership today. That's no surprise since every leader desires a team who will bond together in times of adversity. In dictionary terms, buy-in is the "acceptance of and willingness to actively support and participate in something." In my experience though, that definition falls drastically short of the raw, instinctive commitment inherent in winning organizations.

Buy-in can be fleeting, something people try on for size to see if it fits. It is relatively easy to obtain when spirits are high, but that says little about how it will hold up during times of stress. And as anyone in a competitive business environment knows, today's buy-in is always at risk of being sold to tomorrow's higher bidder.

"Believe-in" runs deeper. It is not a decision but a reflex. It is your core fight-or-flight response when all else is stripped bare. Believe-in is the bond that holds great teams together when the situation screams that everyone should fend for themselves. That makes it far more powerful than buy-in when organizations are truly tested.

Few organizations have ever needed believe-in more than those

Chicago Cubs' Lovable Losers. That's what happens when you haven't won a title in over a century. When we arrive, a subset of devoted fans unwaveringly believes a championship will someday come. The challenge is instilling that same sense of belief in the players and staff who are in a position to make it happen.

Ironically, the Cubs' transformation begins long before the team starts winning. Two simple phrases – one from leadership and one from the players themselves – change everything.

The first phrase is the joint effort of two senior staff members. It starts with Tim Cossins, the Cubs' chief minor league instructor. "Cuz" – as he is invariably known to everyone within roughly 90 seconds of meeting him – is a bundle of persistent positivity. Working mostly with younger players, he is one of the first voices modeling how we hope our minor leaguers will take ownership of their careers.

Cuz's simple message stresses the importance of being ready "when it happens." Not *if* it happens…WHEN IT HAPPENS! He preaches preparing for every possibility both good and bad. Minor league players face daunting odds of carving out a Major League career. No matter how high they advance, Cuz is determined they will be prepared for their greatest moments. More importantly, our players know Cuz is all-in on helping them grow.

That trust is key in any leadership scenario. No leader can inspire followers if those followers don't believe you have their best interests at heart as well. I've been with plenty of teams (*i.e.* companies) spouting slogans meant to connect with players (*i.e.* employees). In fact, most organizations have one. But the better players have a keen sense of which slogans have sincerity attached and which are just another empty catchphrase slapped on a t-shirt or printed on a break room sign.

In this case, anyone within earshot not only hears Cuz's sincerity but feels the unbridled passion behind it. It isn't just buying into what is best for either him or the organization. It is a deeper belief that encouraging the best from every player will benefit the Cubs as a whole. It is a belief Cuz lives 24/7.

The front office member hearing Cuz's message most often is Jason McLeod. As VP of Player Development and Scouting, McLeod is the Chicago-based exec who interacts most with our young players. That also gives him the deepest insight into what makes them tick. It is during one of his many minor league trips where McLeod sees the perfect avenue for connecting Cuz's message back to our Major League group.

In the 1930s, the Cubs built a new set of bleachers and what is now an iconic manual scoreboard at Wrigley Field. As part of that construction, a set of flagpoles was mounted on top of the scoreboard. With Wrigley sitting in the middle of an urban neighborhood, there is a constant flow of foot, car, and train traffic within sight of the ballpark. When the renovation was finished, the team began a tradition of flying a flag to let passersby know the result of its last game. It is a custom proudly continued today. A large blue "W" on a white field is raised after every win, while a white "L" on blue represents a loss.

McLeod identifies an opportunity. That W flag will not just represent a single win. It will stand for "When It Happens." The W will symbolize everything about winning – when an individual makes a play, when a minor league team wins a game, and most importantly *when* the franchise wins a World Series. WHEN IT HAPPENS! It will not just be a catchphrase or marketing pitch. It will be the burgeoning belief system for the entire organization.

Seemingly overnight, that white flag with the blue W is everywhere. It's painted on walls, printed on t-shirts, embroidered on front office pullovers. Anywhere you look from Wrigley Field all the way to the Cubs' academy in the Dominican Republic, that big blue W stares back. Sometimes the words accompany the flag. Sometimes not. It doesn't matter – we all know exactly what it means. Now all we need to do is make it our reality.

As the W makes its way through the system, our youngest players join in with their own inspiration. Some have been selected through the draft, making the Cubs the only professional organization they know. Others are acquired through trades as we strategically swap older players for younger ones meant to improve our future talent. Regardless of their origin, these players see the opportunity available to them in Chicago.

As described earlier, part of "When It Happens" includes each player taking ownership of personal effort and performance. To recognize peers displaying that effort, our youngsters adopt a second motto: "That's Cub!"

Starting at the lower levels, "That's Cub!" soon spreads everywhere. It becomes a battle cry praising teammates for extra effort even if the outcome isn't perfect. Make a diving play. That's Cub! Force an opponent error by hustling on the bases. That's Cub! Finish the game with the dirtiest uniform even if the stats say you had a bad day. That is most definitely Cub.

Other staff take notice. Josh Lifrak, our Mental Skills Director, sees something special. Lifrak has recently joined the Cubs from the famed IMG Sports Academy. Filling what is then a relatively new role in baseball, Lifrak works directly with players and staff on the mental resiliency needed to survive one of the longest and most grueling schedules in all professional sports. Lifrak believes the genuine peer-to-peer support of "That's Cub!" is ideal encouragement, and it is reinforced by the fact our players are so actively looking to give it.

The idea soon expands beyond the field. Before long, "That's Cub!" recognizes behind-the-scenes behavior like work in the weight room, diligence in pregame planning, or even extra time signing autographs for fans. It becomes a badge of honor for going the extra mile in *any* capacity as a player, person, or teammate. As Lifrak would later recall, "Every time someone did something above and beyond, even if it was a player picking up a discarded cup, we would say, 'That's Cub right there!'" Players weren't just embracing individual accountability. They were taking *responsibility* for setting winning standards systemwide.

As the movement grows, the phrase becomes an acronym. "C" becomes *courage*. "U" becomes *urgency*. "B" becomes *belief*. Lifrak explains it as "the courage to do the right thing, the urgency to do it right now, and the belief you are going to get it done." It isn't just buy-in. It's an identity. That belief is embedded in our young players as they swarm up the minor league ladder toward Chicago.

While the world sees "Cub" as lovable losing, our players flip the script. They use Cub to reinforce anything and everything about winning. And it isn't just an artificial tagline. It is a homegrown movement embraced by a group who fully believes in what we are trying to accomplish. We celebrate winning behavior, which in turn incentivizes winning behavior, which in turn creates more winning behavior. That flywheel doesn't just align with "When It Happens." It amplifies it. It is powerful stuff.

In short order, "When It Happens" and "That's Cub!" become foundations for the entire franchise. Once the belief takes hold, results follow. As the winning flows upward, Chicago's Major League team vaults from a miserable 2012 last-place finish to a 2015 playoff appearance and 2016 World Series title. That historic result is led by a group who innately believes in each other, starting with the 45 players who wear a Cub uniform at some point during that championship campaign. And *when it happened*, generations of fans flew that W higher than ever before.

Now *that's* Cub.

Sports has always been a natural storytelling platform for team concepts. But believe-in is not a sports story. It is a human one. While we can occasionally encourage (or even force) buy-in from the top down, its impact on success pales in comparison to believe-in nurtured from the bottom up. Great leaders don't demand buy-in. They build believe-in, a hallmark of elite teams and organizations.

KEY QUESTIONS TO CONSIDER:

- In what area(s) does your organization's believe-in fall short?

- What are the core convictions or beliefs you expect your people to rely on when facing adversity in this area?

- How can you better connect with those beliefs to help achieve your "When It Happens" moment?

READER NOTES

GET COMFORTABLE BEING UNCOMFORTABLE

It comes with the turf.

"To be successful, you must accept all
challenges that come your way.
You can't just accept the ones you like."

– *Mike Gafka, Hewlett Packard executive*

Let's not sugarcoat it – leadership is hard. Anyone who has led for any length of time understands the difficult decisions and uncomfortable tradeoffs that come with the job. But uncomfortable or not, it is leaders who are ultimately responsible for the tough calls no one else wants to make.

One of the most difficult and unfortunately most common leadership tasks is navigating change, especially the need to update a comfortable but broken status quo. This is particularly true when that change is mandated from the very top. While sports often calls the journey going from "worst to first," this uphill climb is an arduous one in any industry.

The truth is no successful change occurs without significant discomfort. That's why Change Management is so much easier in theory than in practice. The best leaders are those who can navigate the messiness while still keeping their teams engaged and intact. Unfortunately, leaders who can't often see their leadership responsibilities passed to someone else.

A prime example in my career occurs when I leave the Cubs for the Seattle Mariners. Just as Theo Epstein was tasked with reversing the futility in Chicago, new Mariners General Manager Jerry Dipoto is expected to do the same in Seattle. Having worked with Jerry before and being familiar with his style, I am offered a senior position to help lead the transition.

While the Mariners lack a catchy nickname like the Loveable Losers, their history is just as frustrating. Since its founding in 1977, Seattle is the only franchise yet to appear in a World Series game – an unfortunate distinction it still holds today. Despite boasting some of the game's biggest stars and a league record 116 regular season wins in 2001, the Mariners have qualified for the playoffs just four times in 39 seasons when we arrive. Its 15-year nonplayoff streak is among the longest in North American pro sports at the time. It isn't lovable losing. It's entrenched mediocrity.

The initial mechanics of the change are very similar to Chicago – a preliminary programs assessment followed by a first set of adjustments. With the Cubs those adjustments were tackled with a focused, determined style based on clear communication and decisive action. The initial Mariner mindset is much different.

Baseball, like most businesses, moves through a predictable annual cycle. While not as structured as say a publicly traded company issuing quarterly and annual reports, baseball has natural pauses letting teams step back, assess, and begin making necessary changes. The midseason All-Star break is one of those pauses. Coming out of that break his first year in charge, Jerry gathers the team's leadership group in a large conference room at our home stadium. The attendees include Directors and above in all areas of team operations. All three scouting departments – amateur players, professional players, and international players – are represented. Jerry is the voice at the head of the table. I am seated at the foot. The remaining junior and senior leaders are scattered in between.

As usual, the Mariners aren't doing much in the standings. While plenty of season remains, our Major League team, minor league affiliates, and third-party rankings of young players have all drifted to their customary middle-of-the-pack spot. It is a continuation of the lackluster performance we've been brought in to address.

Jerry opens by acknowledging the team's recent history and reemphasizing ownership's desire for change. No one in the room is to blame for the past, but this is the group responsible for charting the future. The sole purpose of this meeting is rolling up our shirt sleeves and beginning the hard work of getting better.

The first few topics are standard forays into policy and procedure. Yes, we will do some things differently, but none are radical departures from industry norms. These discussions encounter little friction. The bigger and more important conversation is which staff members can help us perform at a championship level. Jerry frames it succinctly. If we want to be a top franchise, we need the best possible people at every level on and off the field.

That introduction leads us directly into the messiest mess of any sizable turnaround – who stays and who goes. No organization in any industry completes a worst-to-first journey with the exact same set of employees. There is no reason to think this Seattle group will be the first.

Jerry starts the discussion with, "As we head into the second half, what changes might we need to consider on our current staff?"

Our new Director of Player Development goes first. Having spent several months reviewing our system, he gives a detailed breakdown of our minor league coaches and support staff. He identifies early strengths and weaknesses with the initial skills gaps we need to close. The second half of the season will bring more information, but the checkpoints are in place to make appropriate staffing decisions at the end of the year. It's a pragmatic evaluation, and we unsurprisingly have work to do.

When we turn to scouting, however, it is clear our holdover leadership has little stomach for this part of the conversation. After a long and awkward silence in which no one volunteers to start, Jerry singles out the Amateur Director for his opinion. We hear a long, wandering answer on some vague areas for improvement. If nothing else, his repetition of some earlier buzzwords shows the meeting's purpose has not been missed.

"That's great," Jerry says. "Do we have the right scouts to do this?"

Another pause. "Umm…no."

"Who falls short?"

The Director's answer suggests there are a few underperforming scouts but does not include any names.

Jerry frowns. "Okay. Who?"

Another non-answer. Patience thinning, Jerry tries a different angle.

"Well, how much of the staff might we need to turn over?"

After a moment of thought, the Director replies that a quarter of his staff might need to be replaced to build a top group. We don't have specifics yet, but at least it's a start.

Visibly annoyed, Jerry turns to International Scouting. Sensing the mood, the International Director expresses the same general points. Before being asked, he offers his own turnover rate of "maybe one-third" of the department's staff. When Jerry requests a name for replacement, the Director says he knows one is needed but wants time to think about it given the obvious importance of the decision. Jerry doesn't seem pleased with this answer, but after a few moments decides to let it slide. There's visible relief when he moves on.

The Pro Director finishes the scouting review with the same generic suggestions. Once again, no names are offered, but in what is becoming a disturbing trend he suggests "up to half" our pro staff might need to turn over to build a top-flight group. Half. I'm stunned at the figure.

I glance at my notes. According to our own directors, at least a couple dozen of roughly 75 scouts might need to be replaced to build a championship group. And these aren't outside critiques. These are estimates being given by the directors who built these staffs in the first place. I'm feeling a little queasy. *How in the world had this been allowed to happen?!?* Of course, the next step is connecting these numbers to names. Ugh.

With that idea in mind, Jerry circles back. I'll give him credit. I've known Jerry a long time, and one thing he has always done is let his directors direct. The problem here is no one's directing. At all. You can't call yourself a decision maker if you won't actually make decisions, especially in a business as competitive as this one. With the International Director's "let me think about it" having worked before, all three rally around the idea of getting more time to come up with an answer. Jerry's frown is joined by a clenched jaw.

At this point, the frustration isn't just about evasive answers. It's a clash between Jerry's leadership expectations and those of the previous regime. The prior group wanted department heads to sit quietly and keep things in check until receiving their next order. Jerry wants managers to step up and take charge. That gap in expectations – and more importantly the skillset required to meet them – is now on full display.

With the room becoming increasingly uncomfortable, there's a knock at the door. A Media Relations assistant steps in to remind Jerry about an appearance on the pre-game radio show. Clearly dissatisfied, Jerry leans into the table over pressed palms and sharply declares, "Be prepared to pick this up first thing tomorrow." He then pushes himself up, glares at the group, and stalks out of the room.

His departure releases the pressure. The room exhales, and with the bullet temporarily dodged people start moving to pack their bags.

"One second," I say scanning my notepad. "Let me make sure I have this straight. We're saying we need to roll over a quarter of our amateur staff, a third of our international staff, and up to half our pro staff but aren't ready to discuss a single name?"

After some awkward shifting, the Pro Director finally offers, "I was thinking more in terms of a five-year plan." There are no other responses.

My immediate thought is Theo Epstein declaring in Chicago that five-year plans are bullshit. I now understand why. It's a built-in excuse for avoiding difficult decisions. After all, why make a tough choice today if the timeline easily lets us bump it to tomorrow? That is *exactly* what is happening here. The problem is too much delay eventually runs you out of time. With this meeting only lasting a few days, we can't afford to push this conversation until the next time everyone's schedules align.

Realizing Theo's blunt assessment is probably not my best strategy, I instead ask, "Oh. Do you have a five-year contract?"

Another awkward pause. "No."

"Neither do I."

More silence.

It is a frustrating moment. We need urgency, not a five-year escape plan. We've admitted we need to make changes, but it is clear we aren't ready to offer any specifics. So, I take a different approach.

"We still have time before dinner," I say, "Let's try something else. What are the better scouting groups in baseball doing we might be able to do here? Who are the best teams in your areas right now?"

The International Director starts the conversation by naming the Texas Rangers, who deserve a special shoutout even now because they really did dominate the international scene at the time. He mentions the New York Yankees along with a couple other clubs.

The Amateur Director goes next. He cites the Los Angeles Dodgers – also well deserved – then adds "and I'm not saying this because you are in the room, but I'd definitely put the Cubs near the top of the list."

Lastly, the Pro Director chimes in. The Houston Astros top his list with the St. Louis Cardinals third, which makes sense since the Astros' General Manager at the time had a huge influence over the Cardinal program in a prior role. The Director slots the Cubs in between with the same disclaimer that Chicago is not that high simply because I am in the room.

While this wasn't the intent, I see an opening. I don't need to ask what they think those clubs might be doing that Seattle isn't. I can simply tell them since I helped build the system for the only team named twice.

"Okay," I say, "Let me ask you this. Would the Cubs have made your list five or six years ago?"

The Amateur Director literally laughs out loud. "No way!" he chuckles. "They were *never* a group we worried about a few years ago. You guys did a great job turning that around."

"Thanks," I reply. "But I'm not with 'those guys' anymore. I'm here. And for what it's worth, one thing I *know* helped turn that around was not ducking decisions in meetings like this. We made the best choice we could and moved on. If we can't do that here, ownership will put someone else in this room…and probably sooner than five years. I'd prefer that not happen."

With that impassioned speech fully delivered, we break for dinner. But the mood is subdued. Compared to most of our meals, it's a muted affair with limited conversation.

Staying true to his word, Jerry jumps right back into staffing the next morning. The tension is immediate. Ten minutes in, we have plenty of pleas for additional time but not a single name. Oh well, so much for my inspirational words the afternoon before.

Clearly aggravated now, Jerry suggests a name for dismissal. It is an obvious candidate, a scout who had physically threatened a colleague over a simple and very standard difference of opinion a few months prior. It was a scout whose temper had already gotten him terminated from another club. The most recent incident was serious enough to notify the Mariners' Human Resources department, and the scout's contract is up at the end of the year. If there was ever an easy leadership call, this is it.

Yet somehow, we remain stuck. Awaiting a response, the silence only grows louder. Jerry's clenched jaw is now accompanied by a disgusted stare. With our dismissal candidate on the pro staff, it is obvious who we are waiting on. Finally, the Pro Director looks down at his hands and mumbles, "That feels a little hasty."

"A little hasty?!?" Jerry counters. "He threatened a coworker!"

In a lower voice and almost plaintively, "I believe in second chances."

At this point, Jerry doesn't even try to hide his anger. "Fine," he snaps. "You can give him a second chance. But let me be clear, his future is attached to yours. If he sinks, you sink too!"

The outburst slaps the room to attention. Anyone with even the slightest slouch is now sitting ramrod straight.

The Pro Director stammers, "Wait! What?!? I don't want his job attached to mine!"

"You're not getting it," Jerry says in a lower voice but through gritted teeth. "You. Are. The. Director. You pick your staff. Being attached to that staff is part of the gig. That's the way it works. So, what would you like to do?"

After one final hesitation, a muffled "I think we need a new scout."

With that, we have our first name. Slowly but surely, others emerge to start the much-needed discussion of where we stack up and where we fall short. The Scouting Department comments aren't nearly as thorough as the Player Development review, but we are at least creeping in the right direction. Finally.

Did we make as many tough calls as we should have that first year? Being honest, no. In fact, there's an argument we likely delayed the eventual turnaround. Ironically, by the time the Mariners finally ended that non-playoff streak at twenty seasons, those initial turnover estimates weren't far off. A handful of scouts left on their own, but more were displaced by the unyielding need to improve in an industry where the scoreboard tells you exactly where you stand. Surprisingly – or maybe not – a subset of those changes included the three scouting directors in the room that fateful day. This not only underscores the importance of finding the right leaders but also proves the broader point: if you are someone who chooses not to lead, most companies have no choice but to find someone who will.

As I said at the top, leadership is hard. As are the tradeoffs that come with it. In my experience, the toughest tradeoff of all is balancing our need to feel comfortable with the often uncomfortable obligation to do the right thing. As leaders, we never want to forfeit our capacity for empathy, kindness, or understanding. At the same time, we can never lose sight of our responsibility to do right by our people and organizations. The consolation is leaders who find the right mix are often liked simply for their willingness to do uncomfortable things.

KEY QUESTIONS TO CONSIDER:

- What uncomfortable issue do you know you or your organization must confront but keeps avoiding?
- What opportunities are you foregoing or additional risks are you taking on by not addressing this issue?
- What adjustments to mindset, resources, or people will allow you to make the tough calls needed to start this journey?

READER NOTES

PRINCIPLE EIGHT
MASTER YOUR INFORMATION

Be sure to leverage ALL of it.

"If a magic fairy instantly gave you
absolutely all the information resources
the company would ever need, do you
think people would instantly know
what to do with it and how to use it well?"

– Peter G. W. Keen, author and speaker

"We have to be data-driven!"

It's a rallying cry of modern business. Metrics abound, and the pace of information will only accelerate as artificial intelligence joins the fray. Like baseball's WAR ("Wins Above Replacement") or basketball's VORP ("Value Over Replacement Player"), today's businesses are awash in an ever-creeping wave of acronyms:

- KPI (Key Performance Indicator)
- OKR (Objectives and Key Results)
- NPS (Net Promoter Score)
- ARR (Annual Recurring Revenue)
- CAC (Customer Acquisition Cost)

The problem today isn't gathering or storing this data. It's consistently converting it into better decisions. The challenge lies in merging hard data with more subjective inputs like experience, observation, and intuition. We know the objective and subjective both matter. The art is in how we blend them. Just as blindly following data risks undervaluing common sense, ignoring data that contradicts our gut is equally dangerous. The goal is using *all* the information at our disposal to make smarter decisions. The better we master our information, the greater our chances of success.

Surprisingly, my most memorable power-of-information moment came not in a baseball stadium but at a hockey arena instead. Late in my career, I was invited to attend three days of scouting meetings with a National Hockey League team. The goal was to exchange best practices and ideas, particularly regarding analytics in player evaluation.

In professional sports, baseball is generally recognized for analytical expertise. Mind you, this is not because baseball is necessarily more progressive or open-minded. It is simply the first sport forced to embrace analytics as a competitive edge. In fact, the early days of baseball's messy, often combative analytics shift are famously portrayed in Michael Lewis's bestseller *Moneyball*.

Baseball's analytic advantage is due to the game unfolding in so many discrete, measurable moments. Each pitcher's biomechanical movements can be recorded before the ball leaves his hand. The ball's velocity, shape, and exact location are then tracked as it travels to the plate. At the plate, the hitter's biomechanics are collected along with the impact, speed, and trajectory of any ball put into play. That leads to reaction times and angles for every fielder. The game's natural rhythm produces dozens of datasets which can be analyzed individually or in combination to assess their impact on game results.

Sports with a more continuous flow – football, soccer, basketball, hockey, etc. – do not have that luxury. Not only are independent datasets more difficult to obtain, but the added complexity of player interactions makes it harder to separate cause and effect.

That makes any analytic insights in these sports more directional than exact.

The invitation here is meant to see which broad baseball insights might translate to the NHL. And I stress those insights will be broad. Other than knowing a Left Wing is on the left and a Right Wing is on the right, I am well out of my depth on the player intricacies needed to perform at hockey's highest level.

But there is also an urgency behind the ask. This team is near the bottom of the standings, which means it is guaranteed one of the first few picks in the upcoming draft. Get the pick right, and they might build a future contender. Get it wrong, and heads might roll. The stakes cannot be clearer.

Walking into the room, everyone knows a "baseball guy" has been invited. Introducing myself, I immediately admit my lack of hockey knowledge. But I also point out I have more than enough airline miles, hotel stays, and player mistakes of my own to appreciate how difficult their job is. I can only hope to add something useful the next three days.

It doesn't take long to notice the similarities between baseball and hockey discussions. The lingo is different, but the personalities and communication quirks are identical. Scouts are inherently territorial. They argue for what they know best. But regardless of the argument, management's job is to filter the noise and find the truth.

The biases in most scouting meetings start with turf (think of sales and operations immediately staking out positions in almost any joint meeting). In baseball, tensions can arise when a scout from say California comments on a player from the East Coast, especially if those observations come in a brief look. It is the same when a scout from Florida offers notes on a West Coast player. The local scouts can't wait to pounce on any perceived flaws in this "outside" perspective. In the early stages of my career, these disagreements often devolved into fiery shouting matches. One of the major benefits of analytics over the years has been creating more rational baselines for player evaluation.

Hockey's divide pits North America and Europe. Anytime a scout from one region speaks about a player from the other, the locals noticeably stiffen. And just like baseball, most follow up comments from the locals contain as much rebuttal as consideration for the opinion just provided. In the first few players discussed, there is little signal to help lessen the noise.

Except there *is* signal. We just aren't using it. With each new player, the team's analytics department displays a simple bar graph with a set of metrics. Each bar represents the percentile ranking of the player's skill in relation to the rest of the class. The higher the bar, the better the player's performance. The lower the bar, the greater the potential problem. The categories are simple enough even a hockey novice like me can follow along: quality offensive and defensive plays, passing efficiency, loose puck battles, shots, and shots from the slot (a more effective scoring area). Despite graphs being shown for every prospect so far, we haven't directly referenced even one.

The pivotal moment comes in a tense debate about a European defenseman, a high-profile teenager expected to be chosen early in the draft. That makes him a legitimate candidate for the team's first pick. He has high-end ability and athleticism. However, he plays a raw, unpolished game that will require plenty of development patience from the team selecting him. It is your typical high-risk/high-reward business decision. The challenge − as always − is making a smart one.

The scouting director works his way around the room asking each scout who saw the player to comment on his potential. The final comments come from a roughly 60-year-old scout I'll call Chris. Based in western Canada, Chris is clearly a respected voice in the room. He watched the player at the annual Hlinka Gretzky Cup, a premier international tournament showcasing the best under-18 players in the world. As live looks go, the Hlinka Gretzky is about as competitive an environment you can find for gauging a player's performance.

"Hey, Chris," the director calls across the room, "You saw this kid, right?"

"Yeah," Chris replies.

The European scouts snap to attention, unsure what Chris the Canadian is going to say next. Chris presents his notes. He speaks highly of the player's skating and passing skills. He also likes the player's ability to drive play up and down the ice. Chris is not as sold on the player's defensive positioning or willingness to engage in the more physical parts of the game.

"I think this kid could be a quality offensive defenseman in the NHL," Chris concludes. "But remember, I only saw him for a game and a half."

It's not the strongest endorsement, but it's an honest one given the brevity of Chris's look. When he finishes, yet another ignored bar graph fades from the wall as we move to the next name.

I decide now is the time to raise my hand. This is not some obscure player from the depths of the draft. This is a premium talent who will command millions of dollars. Unfortunately, he also fits a profile where the historic outcomes range from glory to disaster. This is the type of player who makes or breaks scouting departments. That also makes it a player you'd better get right.

Choosing my words carefully, I say, "If I can make an observation, I can't help but notice we keep putting up analytics graphs but haven't actually used one yet."

I see some surprised faces as the room realizes that is indeed the case. I also see a look screaming "*Finally!*" on the face of the junior analyst who has been diligently running the screen.

I turn toward Chris. "Hey, I've been there. You're watching this kid, but he's not from your region. You like what you see, but you have very little background to work with. You see a game and a half but have no idea if this is his best game and a half ever, his worst game and a half ever, or a clean look at what he can actually do."

"Exactly!" Chris exclaims with a look of relief on his face.

"But we *do* have more information to help sort him out," I say. "Chris, if you had to guess at this kid's analytics graph, what do you think it would look like? Quality offensive plays, high or low?"

"Oh, definitely high."

"Defensive plays?"

"That would be low."

"Passing?"

"Way high!"

"Loose puck battles?"

Chris thinks a moment, "50/50. Halfway."

After rattling off the rest of the listed metrics, I ask the analyst to put the player's graph back on the screen. The bar heights match Chris's observations perfectly.

"You nailed his graph," I say pointing at the screen, "Which means your game and a half pretty much mirrors what he's done all year."

I turn to the analyst, "How many games is this?"

After a couple quick clicks, the analyst replies, "Forty-three."

"Forty-three," I repeat turning back to Chris. "So, your game and half matches *forty-three games* worth of data. And this isn't a scout from another team throwing out a hot take at the airport. This data has been collected all season long to help make better decisions into the draft."

I pause for a second before nodding toward the graph, "Our entire job as evaluators is building enough conviction to feel we are properly presenting a player to the room. Based on this, where's your conviction now?"

With an almost shocked look and noticeably more confident tone, Chris answers, "My conviction is *waaaay* higher. In fact, if I could, I'd move this player higher on my list."

The entire room looks my way. Shrugging my shoulders, I say, "I can't tell you if you can move him. All I can say is in our meetings we want scouts' latest opinions using the latest info. Any time that opinion changes, we change our list. No one wants to present a player incorrectly in a meeting like this. The job's hard enough as it is."

Heads snap the other way as the director proclaims, "Put him where he belongs! I don't care how he gets there. I only want to get him right."

That closing exchange leads into a short break. As most of the room files into the hallway, Chris beelines for my seat. Clearly agitated, he throws up his hands and says, "That was easy! How come no one's ever explained that to me before?!?"

"I don't know," I reply with a grin, "But it's being explained now. Baseball's just had longer to figure it out."

"Those graphs make total sense. Why don't they just give them to us for every player?"

In fairness, Chris's question is a natural reaction for anyone first recognizing the power of analytics. However, it also marks a risky moment in adopting them. The temptation is to treat analytics as a standalone answer rather than a tool for deeper insight. In reality, analytics most often work best as a complement to and not a replacement for other sources of information. This is especially true in industries like pro sports where analytics provide directional clues at best.

"Well," I reply, "they don't give you the graphs for two reasons. One, just like it takes you time to build history on a player, it took 43 games to build that graph. Two, if they just give you the graphs, you'll see exactly what the analytics tell you to see when you get to the rink. Analytics only tell us *what* a player does. You tell us *how* he does it. We need both to figure out what parts of his game will translate to the NHL. The point is crosschecking everything as we go."

I've come to learn this crosschecking function is where premier organizations excel in any industry. They have detailed processes for cross-referencing objective and subjective information. They also understand not only the numbers but the concepts and behaviors behind them. When the two match, pat yourself on the back and keep going. When they don't, it is not time to pick a side and duke it out (which is exactly what happens in more industries than we'd like to admit). Instead, it is time to put *all* your information on the table to determine the cause of the discrepancy. Identifying those causes and adjusting accordingly is what separates good organizations from great ones.

Over the next three days, Chris drifts over almost every break. Routinely asked to evaluate players in abbreviated looks, he now fully appreciates how analytics can augment his observations. As time goes on, he brings others into the conversation. We swap notes on how data can help with evaluations, rankings, and even scheduling when the calendar gets tight. The hockey guys learn a lot about the basics of balancing information. The baseball guy learns just as much about the nuance of that balance in their world. We're all surprised at just how cleanly the bulk of it transfers.

Having now observed that power of information moment in several industries, I'm no longer surprised. I've learned of more productive farms pairing cutting edge sensors with the insights of fourth-generation farmers. City infrastructures improved by blending the latest metrics with the observations of experienced plant managers. Neighborhoods made safer by leveraging artificial intelligence with the input of police officers in the field.

The best organizations don't just collect information. They know how to balance it. Data without intuition is rigid. Intuition without data is reckless. The organizations who master both? Those are the ones who usually find themselves sitting at the top of their industry standings.

KEY QUESTIONS TO CONSIDER:

- What total information both objective and subjective is available to make decisions in your organization?
- How well has your organization identified and discussed the proper weight for each input when connecting them together?
- What are the most obvious ways your organization can better balance and cross-reference your total information to produce better outcomes?

READER NOTES

WISDOM BEATS EXPERIENCE

Know which you're getting.

"To have lived long does not necessarily imply the gathering of much wisdom…"

– *Paul Eldridge, poet and novelist*

Companies today pour time, effort, and – let's face it – tons of money into finding the right mix of skills and experience. We all crave employees fluent in the latest techniques, yet we also want workers with long histories of success. Every organization appreciates the power of pairing cutting-edge tactics with time-tested expertise. But striking that balance? That's where things get tricky.

Part of the problem lies in semantics. While we say we want "experience," that's not entirely accurate. Regardless of industry, experience presents itself in one of two ways. The first is found in veteran employees whose experience matures into wisdom. They listen well, ask insightful questions, and adapt as needed. The second comes from stagnant employees whose experience deteriorates into stubbornness. They dismiss ideas, cling to past practices, and are often hostile to change. That makes it vital to know which type of experience you are adding to your teams.

In business buzz-speak, it's the difference between introducing a growth or fixed mindset. Growth mindsets engage with teammates by seeking feedback, persisting through setbacks, and enjoying the thrill of a new challenge. They consistently share in ways that move teams forward. Fixed mindsets see limited potential, consider extra effort pointless, and openly avoid tasks outside their comfort zone. Their contributions tend to hold teams back. For any company looking to flourish or achieve, the difference in impact can be enormous.

Think of it like a family reunion. Every family has an Aunt Mary and Uncle Mike. When Aunt Mary walks in, everyone lights up. You can't wait to hear what she's been up to. You're already smiling about the upcoming conversation, even if you have no idea where it will go. Heck, you might even ask for advice on that problem that's been bothering you lately. Aunt Mary's seen a lot over the years but is always open to new ideas, which makes her a great sounding board.

Five minutes later, in strolls Uncle Mike. Everyone turns away when he enters the room. You have no interest in hearing his latest complaint. You already dread rehashing the same gripe he's held the last five reunions. And you're certainly not going to ask for any counsel or advice. He'll only make you feel worse. In fact, you're hoping to avoid him altogether.

As I've often told experienced employees – and I would place myself in that bucket – we get to choose which persona we fill. Principle Two (*People Drive Process*) detailed an Uncle Mike moment, a long-tenured scout who became so rigid and disruptive in our draft room that we were forced to let him go. This chapter is the more likable tale of a 6-foot-3, 250-pound Aunt Mary.

Terry Kennedy was a Major League catcher for 14 seasons. Named to four All-Star games during his career, he also won a prestigious Silver Slugger Award in 1983 as the National League's best-hitting catcher. Stacking his career against the more than 23,000 players who have graced a Major League field, Terry was not just a high performer but an elite one.

Upon retiring as a player, Terry became a distinguished coach and manager. For the next decade-plus, he shared his considerable hitting, catching, and game management knowledge with the next generation of players. With a career pushing close to 30 years, he was an established and widely respected industry voice.

Yet those accomplishments omit a significant part of Terry's baseball pedigree – his father Bob. Bob Kennedy had his own lengthy career, appearing in 16 Major League seasons from 1939 to 1957, including a 3-year interruption for military service during World War II. When his playing career ended, Bob spent another three decades in baseball. After stints as a scout, minor league manager, and director of player development, he served as Major League manager for the Chicago Cubs and Oakland Athletics. Bob reached his professional pinnacle when he was named Cubs' General Manager in 1976. He held that role until 1981, which just happens to be the year of Terry's Major League playing debut. When it comes to depth of knowledge at baseball's highest level, there might not be a more accomplished father-son duo than the Kennedys.

So, when Terry is recommended for an open scouting position on my staff in Chicago, I am immediately intrigued. From the day I arrived, reworking our staff has been a priority. A big part of that revamp is getting the right mix of backgrounds. While scouts mostly work alone, the group collaborates quite frequently. Knowing that, I want a staff where our collective experience can help answer any individual question. So far, so good. Our group includes two former front office executives, three scouts with extensive amateur experience, a former Major League pitcher, and two younger scouts with the potential to grow into larger roles. We also have a parttime scout with a decades-long college coaching career. What we don't have is a former Major League position player or someone with deep professional coaching experience. Terry ticks both boxes. The risk, of course, is he has never scouted before. Yes, he has experience, but that experience is only valuable if Terry can transition to the new role and contribute in a way that strengthens the team.

Our first conversation is over the phone. After three decades on the field, what makes Terry want to watch from the stands? He briefly explains the beating his 6-foot-3 frame has taken from all those years squatting down, blocking pitches, and absorbing collisions with baserunners. That wear and tear has been compounded by riding buses and running pregame drills as a minor league instructor. Terry still enjoys the camaraderie and loves the game. He just wants to contribute in a less physically demanding role.

Our second interview is over dinner in Arizona. In business terms, we often talk about cross-functional skills. In baseball terms, this conversation is about as cross-functional as it gets. Terry asks as many questions as he answers. He possesses not only firsthand playing and coaching knowledge but an indirect executive's perspective from all those years watching Bob. Terry remembers his father scribbling scouting reports at the kitchen table. He recalls conversations about players, trades, and roster decisions. The problem is Terry has never put those experiences into scouting terms before. My initial impression is a high-level thinker with an obvious eye for the game. On paper, his skills are a great fit for our staff.

Back in Chicago, I realize there is an item I didn't address. Despite his impressive background, Terry would be an entry-level scout. That means entry-level mistakes. He's been in supervisory positions a long time. This would be a brand-new role overseen by a first-time director fifteen years his junior. How will that work when the inevitable mistakes occur?

I call Terry and tell him I need another piece of information.

"What's that?" he asks.

"Well," I say, "if we bring you on board, you'll be a rookie scout."

"Correct."

"Do you remember when you were a rookie player and the manager called you in for feedback?"

"Yes."

"And your rookie manager days when the farm director did the same?"

"Yeeeess…I see where you're going with this. As a rookie scout, would that feedback come from you?"

"Mostly, yes," I reply, "and in my experience it's always better for rookies to ask for feedback rather than wait for a problem to arise."

"That's been my experience too," Terry says, "That won't be a problem."

And with that, we have a new scout.

About two weeks into his scouting career, Terry gives me a call from a Cleveland hotel. "It's your rookie scout," he chuckles, "and I think I need some feedback."

"What's that?" I reply with a grin.

"I think I want to put an 80 on Corey Kluber's curveball."

For context, scouts traditionally use a sliding 20 to 80 scale when grading a player's abilities in a subset of categories. A grade of 50 represents Major League average. Those numbers are often paired with verbal descriptions ensuring all evaluators are on the same page with what they are describing. On our pitching scale, a 50 is regarded as competitive against Major League hitters even over the heart of the plate. A bottom-of-the-scale 20 has zero Major League value while a top-end 80 means the whole stadium knows the pitch is coming yet the hitter still can't hit it. For the statistically inclined, an 80 is roughly three standard deviations above average. So, rarefied air.

This is an early test of putting Terry's experience to use.

"Wow," I say, "That's a big grade. You caught and hit against a lot of Major League curveballs. Whose was better?"

After a slight pause but no real hesitation, Terry replies, "Bert Blyleven's and Nolan Ryan's."

I pause. "That's it?"

"Yup."

"So, two Hall of Famers with arguably the best curveballs of the last 25 years. Got it. Do you have Kluber's player page up on your computer?"

"Yes."

"What do his analytics say?"

Scouting analytics are new for Terry. They are also the steepest part of the learning curve for most rookie scouts. We always want to double check the narrative our eyes suggest against the data available to support or question our observation. But you need to know how to interpret it. This is the area we've spent the most time getting Terry up to speed. It is also the area he's had the fewest reps and been slowest to incorporate. Carefully, he talks through the information in front of him.

"Let's see...he throws it for plenty of strikes...hitters rarely make contact against it…and when they do, their results are terrible." There's a pause before he adds, "It's an 80. Got it." I can feel the smile on the other end of the line.

"Great. Have a nice day."

Hanging up, I know Terry Kennedy isn't just a heck of a player and a heck of a manager but has the chance to be a heck of a scout. And that's exactly what happened. Terry scouted another seven years before retiring in full, giving him a total of 38 as a player, coach, manager, and scout. Over that span, he made himself a valuable resource and trusted thought partner in just about every facet of the game. And much of that trust came from the fact he was just as curious about getting feedback as giving it. Whether a rookie scout or seasoned exec, you always knew you were in for a relaxed, informative exchange. Even now, you'd be hard pressed to find anyone knowing Terry who doesn't break into a grin when hearing his name.

But those grins have little to do with his playing, coaching, or scouting *experience*. They come instead from the industry *wisdom* he so freely shared along the way. In the end, Terry Kennedy turned out to be one heck of an Aunt Mary.

We all know experience matters. The lesson here is regardless of industry the *type* of experience matters more. Whenever your team needs a dose of experience, take the extra time to find your Aunt Mary. The wisdom she brings will greatly increase your chances of success.

KEY QUESTIONS TO CONSIDER:

- Who are the experienced voices expected to positively impact your organization's conversations?
- How effective are these voices in presenting their experience as wisdom rather than stubbornness? (And if you are an experienced voice, how effectively are you riding this line?)
- How do you ensure Aunt Mary participates in as many conversations as possible?

READER NOTES

THE FINAL SCORE
PUT 'EM ALL TOGETHER

Let your forces multiply.

"Great things are not done by impulse, but by
a series of small things brought together."

— Vincent Van Gogh, 19th-century artist

Winning at the highest levels isn't just hard. It's intricate. High-level success can't be achieved by mastering a single principle alone. It instead requires embedding *all* your principles into the processes and behaviors that drive success. It's the art of knowing which principle to apply when even as you learn new ones along the way.

The most successful leaders and organizations apply their principles in a way that creates a *force-multiplier effect*. A concept borrowed from military science, *force multiplication* occurs when a combination of personnel or resources will achieve a more successful outcome than using one in isolation. In business terms, force multiplication means layering principles in a way that pushes your organization to greater heights than applying a single principle alone.

I met the most successful force multiplier of my career in the triple-digit heat of a Texas minor league ballpark. The game was still hours away, but I was there to watch pregame practice. Despite the early arrival, another scout has beaten me there. He's tucked into the upper corner of the stands, one of the few shady spots out of the blazing heat. I head over to introduce myself (and admittedly steal some of that shade). He's short, stocky, and at least a couple of decades my senior. Wearing dark sunglasses under a wide-brimmed hat, he is intently scribbling notes on an old-school yellow legal pad.

I walk over and stick out my hand, "Joe Bohringer."

He looks up from his notes and returns the handshake, "Jerry Krause."

And just like that, I find myself sitting next to a 70-year-old basketball Hall of Famer.

Most who recognize the name know Jerry Krause as the architect of the Chicago Bulls' basketball dynasty. Those Bulls won six NBA championships in eight stormy seasons from 1991 to 1998. They were famously led by Michael Jordan, a fierce competitor widely recognized as one of the best if not *the* best player to ever pick up a basketball.

What most fans don't know is Jerry also made a name in baseball. When starting his career in the early 1960s, it was hard for scouts in any sport to earn a full-time living. Jerry solved this problem by pulling double duty. He crisscrossed the Midwest during the fall and winter evaluating young basketball players before hitting those same roads again to watch baseball in the spring and summer. He spent most of the 1970s and early '80s as a baseball executive before switching over to lead the Bulls from 1985 to 2003.

After earning those six NBA titles and a banner with his name on it hanging in the Bulls' arena, Jerry returned to baseball in senior scouting roles during the last years of his career. His final record includes work with five NBA and seven MLB teams across six decades. That's a lot of logos worn – and a lot of principles learned.

That unexpected meeting led to countless hours discussing players, staffing, team building, and organizational structure with Jerry. Dozens of conversations in ballparks, hotels, and even his homes in Chicago and Arizona. I realize he has his public detractors, but my interactions were always positive. He willingly and openly shared his experiences, and his record of success is undeniable. I didn't bump into just another scout that hot Texas day. I met a walking encyclopedia of winning people, programs, and principles. And nowhere did Jerry's principles multiply more forcefully than that historic NBA run in Chicago. In fact, he forged *all* of them together to help build a dynasty.

Principle One: Winning Is Not Normal.

Krause joined the Bulls directly from a successful stint with baseball's Chicago White Sox. The Sox were owned by local businessman Jerry Reinsdorf. Krause was an executive who helped overhaul those White Sox from non-contenders to a 1983 division title, the team's first playoff appearance in 24 years. A passionate fan, Reinsdorf expanded his sports portfolio by purchasing basketball's Bulls in early 1985. Reinsdorf's first move as an NBA owner was walking into the White Sox offices and telling Krause to pack his things. He was moving across town to run the struggling Bulls.

While the Bulls had a promising young star in 22-year-old Michael Jordan, the team was mired in the bottom half of the standings and hadn't been a serious contender in over a decade. Krause's mandate was recreating the White Sox' worst-to-first overhaul, except in a different league playing a different sport. Walking in the door, little about the Bulls screamed winner. Krause's job was to reset that mentality from the ground up.

Principle Two: People Drive Process.

Jerry knew the right coaches were key to the environment he wanted to create. That search led to two bold yet unconventional hires. The first was Tex Winter. Tex was a long-time college coach best known for pioneering the Triangle Offense, an innovative and unusual system featuring heavy ball movement to create scoring opportunities. His teams menaced college basketball for over three decades, including winning nearly 70% of his games in fifteen years as head coach at Kansas State. However, Winter and his system failed miserably in his one prior shot as an NBA coach.

Despite that failure, Jerry remained intrigued by the Triangle Offense. He felt it could work in the NBA, especially if built around a talent like Jordan. So shortly after taking over the Bulls, Jerry approached Winter with the idea and convinced him to give the NBA another try. Winter's attention to detail and passion for the system won over the team. Led by Jordan, the Bulls' young offense steadily improved.

With his chief tactician in place, Jerry turned to the head coaching position. That led to Phil Jackson. Having first met while Jackson was a college player in the late 1960s, the two kept in touch while Jackson carved out a journeyman NBA playing career and settled into coaching. Jackson spent several years bouncing around minor leagues in the U.S. and Puerto Rico before Jerry finally hired him as a Bulls assistant in 1987.

Jackson had a reputation for being different, which is part of the reason it took so long for him to land an NBA role. Rather than being steeped in traditional coaching methods, Jackson practiced a more holistic approach. He was a broad thinker fluent in Far Eastern and Native American philosophy. He mixed mindfulness and meditation into pre-game preparation. Many of his ideas were well outside the NBA norm.

Unorthodox or not, Jackson made a huge difference. He helped players get better, which was all that mattered. Yet despite the individual successes, four seasons with "traditional" head coaches still saw the Bulls stuck in the middle of the NBA pack. Jerry decided he had nothing to lose by trying Jackson in the top spot. Skeptics doubted the "hippie guru" had what it took to lead an NBA team. Jerry believed he did.

Two seasons later, the Bulls were NBA champs. In his twenty years as an NBA head coach, Phil Jackson *never* had a losing season. His six titles in Chicago and five more with the Los Angeles Lakers rank him among the winningest coaches of all time in any sport. He was elected to basketball's Hall of Fame in 2007. Winter served as either an assistant coach or consultant for all eleven of those titles, earning him his own Hall of Fame nod in 2011. So, not a bad pair of hires for a couple of coaching vagabonds. Jerry saw beyond any narratives to identify two great people with an uncommon ability to drive process by connecting with players.

Principle Three: Make Championship Demands.

The Bulls' focus on creating a championship environment extended to all areas of the operation. One of the earliest infrastructure changes was creating the NBA's first formal Strength and Conditioning program. In studying best practices across sports, Jerry saw similar programs winning championships in other leagues. This was particularly true in the National Football League, where dedicated strength and conditioning programs had become the norm. The prevailing wisdom was football needed strong, physical players. Basketball didn't. Jerry, however, saw no reason stronger and better-conditioned athletes wouldn't move the Bulls closer to winning.

Unsurprisingly, Bulls' players were skeptical of the new and different approach. What did extra weightlifting and mobility drills have to do with winning basketball games? And wouldn't more intense practices simply leave them tired for games? The skepticism disappeared though as players began seeing improvements, especially the younger ones looking to establish themselves in the league. Jerry recalled how other NBA executives would remark on the Bulls' "luck" in staying healthy during their championship run. He credited this program for much of that advantage. What the Bulls deserve credit for is creating an NBA that demands you be in championship shape before you can reasonably expect to compete for an NBA championship.

Principle Four: Standards Are Not Negotiable.

As the coaching and training changes took hold, Chicago knew it had an up-and-coming team. The missing piece was teaching them how to win. With that in mind, Jerry traded Jordan's close friend Charles Oakley to the New York Knicks for veteran player Bill Cartwright. Jerry felt Cartwright's professionalism would raise the Bulls' standard of play. An angry Jordan felt otherwise. He mockingly labelled Cartwright "Medical Bill" for the time the veteran spent in the training room trying to maintain his aging 7-foot-1 frame. Jordan also made a point of snubbing Cartwright during practices and games. According to the book *The Jordan Rules*, tensions rose to the point Cartwright confronted Jordan directly about his comments and behavior. It was a defining moment. If Jordan and Cartwright couldn't coexist, the trade would be an utter failure.

Fortunately, the confrontation led to an acceptable truce. Cartwright not only became a key member of the Bulls' first three titles but served as co-captain with Jordan as Chicago redefined the NBA's championship standard. In a book written post-retirement, Jordan said, "I was wrong about the Charles Oakley-Bill Cartwright trade…I loved having Charles on the team, but Bill made the difference."

Cartwright made such a difference that when his body finally gave out after those three rings, the Bulls eagerly welcomed him back as an assistant coach. Ever the professional, Cartwright's coaching standards helped him win two more.

Principle Five: Your Culture Is What You Tolerate.

One of the constant phrases I heard from Jerry was "keeping your eyes on the prize." More than just words, that concept was part of the Bulls' DNA. Every decision the organization made was judged against one measure: would it help the team compete for championships? Any person added, process installed, or adjustment made had to clear that bar. If it did, great. If not, it was immediately discarded. Regardless of any risk of criticism or difficulty in execution, nothing was allowed to move the organization further from its goals.

An underrated example is a subtle culture tweak halfway through Chicago's run. The team's first three titles came in consecutive seasons. That was followed by two non-championship years that happened to coincide with Michael Jordan temporarily retiring to give minor league baseball a try. Jordan returned during the second non-title season, but something was missing. The team lacked the same focus and intensity, especially in practice. Bill Cartwright was no longer around, but a lack of veteran presence wasn't the issue. The energy level simply wasn't where the front office and coaching staff believed it needed to be to legitimately compete for an NBA championship. The question was whether this lesser energy level would be tolerated as the team's new normal.

Jerry decided it wouldn't. That offseason he traded for Dennis Rodman, one of the NBA's most controversial personalities. On any given day, you had no idea what clothes, hair color, or new body piercing Rodman might show up with. What you *did* know, however, was his energy level would be through the roof every time he set foot in the arena. Rodman also brought two championships of his own won with the hated-rival Detroit Pistons. There was initial criticism of inserting such a volatile personality into the Bulls' culture, but Rodman turned out to be just the jolt the team needed. He embraced the gritty, gutty, dirty parts of winning basketball, and he did it while practicing and playing all-out all the time. The renewed energy not only vaulted the Bulls back into the league's upper tier but kicked off another string of three straight championships.

Principle Six: Buy-In Is Not Enough.

The Bulls' dynasty is a prime example of the difference between buy-in and believe-in. In any competitive team environment, individual goals are hard to align. There's only one ball on the court, and every individual player craves the chance to show what they can do with it. Consequently, any chance for team success starts by finding shared beliefs the group can rally around.

Off the court, these Bulls are famous – or should I say infamous – for their dysfunctional relationships. Whether it was Krause and Jordan, Jordan and teammate Scottie Pippen, or Jackson and Krause, there are dozens of stories detailing the messy reality of what one sportswriter dubbed "a sports soap opera for the ages." Each of these relationships ended on poor terms in a very public manner. And almost every attempt to document what should be a celebrated era has devolved into rehashing old grievances and reopening old wounds even all these years later.

However, one thing that *can't* be questioned is those teams' shared belief in their ability to win. Almost four dozen players wore a Chicago uniform across those six championships, including some of the game's biggest egos. It was a constant battle to balance individual responsibilities, praise, and compensation with the broader goal of pursuing team wins (sound familiar to any leaders out there?). But regardless of any individual differences, those Bulls' single-minded belief in their ability to compete produced legendary results.

Principle Seven: Get Comfortable
Being Uncomfortable.

Bulls' leadership certainly didn't lack the courage to make uncomfortable decisions, even if against consensus. One such moment came in the 1987 NBA draft. Coming off a disappointing season, the Bulls held the eighth overall pick. One of the more talented players in the draft was Joe Wolf, a former teammate of Jordan's at college basketball powerhouse University of North Carolina. Jordan – by now the league's hottest young star – thought enough of Wolf's ability to praise him in a conversation with ownership. That exchange was passed on to Jerry with the standard disclaimer the choice was still 100% the front office's to make. There was certainly justification for considering Wolf, especially with such a high-profile pick. He was widely considered a first-round talent, and a preexisting relationship with a star player never hurts.

Jerry and his scouts, however, went against the grain by turning the pick into a relative unknown from the University of Central Arkansas, an obscure blip on the college basketball landscape. As a live television audience murmured and groaned in confusion, even commentators admitted, "That's right folks, you probably have never heard of [this player]." This player, Scottie Pippen, posted a Hall of Fame career that includes being named one of the 50 Greatest Players in NBA History. He also happened to serve as Jordan's co-captain for the Bulls' second three crowns. Wolf carved out a lengthy career of his own, but the difference in impact is undeniable. While Scottie Pippen might not have been the comfortable choice, he was most certainly the right one.

Principle Eight: Master Your Information.

The 1990s Bulls were an early model for considering all sources of information. Already trusting Winter and Jackson's nontraditional methods on the court, Jerry relied on Karen Stack Umlauf off it. A former college and pro player herself, Stack Umlauf joined the Bulls to sell tickets the year before Jerry arrived. Familiar with her history, he moved her to the basketball side where she quickly became his conduit for all things basketball.

Those things included interpreting league rules, analyzing film, and even running player workouts. Her information influenced almost every important decision of that championship era. In an industry dominated by men, the Bulls assigned Stack Umlauf responsibilities held by no other woman in the NBA. Jerry didn't care about her gender. He only cared about the quality of her information, which just happened to be among the best around. In many ways it was a precursor to the more diverse, information-is-power front offices prevalent across sports today.

Principle Nine: Wisdom Beats Experience.

In his post-Bulls years, Jerry was incredibly open in sharing the lessons he learned. He repeatedly stressed that most progress happens behind the scenes rather than in front of the cameras. He also freely acknowledged the many messy, unvarnished moments winning requires. His recollections never had a "do it this way" tone but were instead thoughtful, introspective looks at the difficult decisions that come in any high-performing environment. In dozens of conversations on almost every imaginable topic, he never wavered from the importance of finding the right people and doing the right things.

Building those dynasty Bulls was far from a quick fix. It took seven long seasons to win that first championship. Once momentum took hold, however, the next seven seasons produced five more. Jerry made it clear those titles were not the result of any one decision but hundreds of smaller ones crashing, grinding, and eventually building off each other to produce historic results. Those results included dozens of individual accolades, hundreds of millions in team revenue, and a lifelong amount of customer goodwill from the fans who enjoyed that memorable ride. It was force multiplication personified.

Jerry Krause once stated, "Players and coaches alone don't win championships; organizations do." It turns out this insight applies in any competitive industry. Every winning business starts with a collection of driven individuals on a shared quest for continuous improvement. They repeatedly combine, hone, and leverage their core principles into the actions that drive success. But what truly sets winning organizations apart is their leaders' ability to unwaveringly uphold these principles even when – or rather especially when – challenges arise. It is the organizations mastering *that* dynamic who consistently convert winning potential into championship results.

KEY QUESTIONS TO CONSIDER:

- What is the next area of personal or organizational growth you are most passionate about achieving?

- How will you ensure all your core principles are utilized and upheld along the way?

- Whose guidance, support, or partnership do you need to make the most of your journey?

READER NOTES

AFTERWORD

"No matter what discipline you are in – it doesn't matter whether you are a writer, or a basketball player, or a coder – there is a common denominator in how we approach our craft. The attention to detail. The level of commitment. Those things are the same across the board.

So, that is my message: Don't look at what I did but look at how I did it. The how.

And then you can really transfer that over into any profession and any discipline."

– Kobe Bryant, basketball player

The preceding quote is an apt summary of what this book conveys. When it comes to winning – or any success really – it is always easier to identify what we'd like to achieve than how we intend to get there.

While strategy matters, true success is born from passion, conviction, and motivation. Because those are the intrinsic strengths most tested along the way. The principles here not only identify those tests but show how to pass them. If any of the principles seem difficult, it's because they are. All of them. But you now have more tools to conquer them.

If success is your *what*, these principles are the *how*.

All you need to provide is the commitment to put 'em all together.

ACKNOWLEDGMENTS

As with most books, the acknowledgments are plenty. First off, a sincere thank you to everyone I undoubtedly forgot.

Personal thanks to Jerry Dipoto, Mike Hirshfeld, Keith and Christine Kelly, Jerry Krause, Ben Maggio, Dave Malpass, Andy McKay, Gus Quattlebaum, Dan Rubin, Tim Schmidt, and Jerry Weinstein. Each of you contributed not only to this book but to the person I am today.

Professional thanks to Tommy Allison, Jim Benedict, Ken Compton, Howard Darwin, Doc Edwards, Theo Epstein, Bill Geivett, Pat Gillick, Justin Hollander, Jed Hoyer, Terry Kennedy, John McMichen, Layne McWilliams, Mark Mitchke, Saul Rosenthal, Veronica Scarpellino, Matt Slater, Carson Vitale, and Don Welke. I would never have taken this path without the contributions you provided along the way.

Editing thanks to Roger Friedman, Kristina Mangelsdorf, and Stephanie Thompson. I appreciate the extra sets of eyes.

Lastly, a HUGE shout out to the company book club at Lake Cable in Bensenville, Illinois. This book is a million percent better because of their willingness to rip it apart and build it back up in a real-world context. I am forever grateful for the unvarnished honesty (I think).

www.ingramcontent.com/pod-product-compliance
Lightning Source LLC
Chambersburg PA
CBHW071431210326
41597CB00020B/3740